PSYCH STACKED
EMAIL MARKETING

16 UNCONVENTIONAL WAYS TO
PULL MORE MONEY OUT OF YOUR
~~ASS~~ EMAIL LIST

KENNEDY

PSYCH STACKED EMAIL MARKETING

© Copyright 2025 all rights reserved by Kennedy.

This publication may not be reproduced in whole or part in any form without express written permission from the publisher or author.

The book does not represent legal advice or any claims, promises or guarantees. The authors and publishers are not lawyers and cannot offer advice on what is legal where you operate or your niche etc. The authors and publisher are not liable for the outcomes of your actions based on the contents.

DEDICATION

*This book is dedicated to my Dad, Eric
who drove me around to my gigs for years
and only complained a couple of times.*

CONTENTS

CHAPTER 1
UNPOPULAR PSYCHOLOGY   7

CHAPTER 2
YOU PROBABLY WON'T READ THIS BIT   15

CHAPTER 3
MIDDLE FINGER TO THE GURUS   21

CHAPTER 4
LEADS TO ROME   27

CHAPTER 5
HELP! DON'T NURTURE   39

CHAPTER 6
SALES SEQUENCES DON'T MAKE SALES   49

CHAPTER 7
GRANDMOTHER'S FALSE TEETH   59

CHAPTER 8
GRAB THEM BY THE... ATTENTION   69

CHAPTER 9
COLOURING HOOK   81

CHAPTER 10
OFFER PERSISTENCE AND ANGLE PLASTICITY   89

CHAPTER 11
SHORTER, FASTER, BETTER   95

CHAPTER 12
MARKETING IN SPITE OF TECHNOLOGY   105

CHAPTER 13
CUTTING OFF MOST OF THE BUYERS 119

CHAPTER 14
SUBJECT LINES DON'T GET EMAILS OPENED 129

CHAPTER 15
BEWARE OF STRANGERS' MEASURING STICKS 147

CHAPTER 16
DR. FRANKENSTEIN'S BAKERY 161

RESOURCES AND MORE 169
LOOK WHO'S TALKING 171
ACKNOWLEDGEMENTS 173

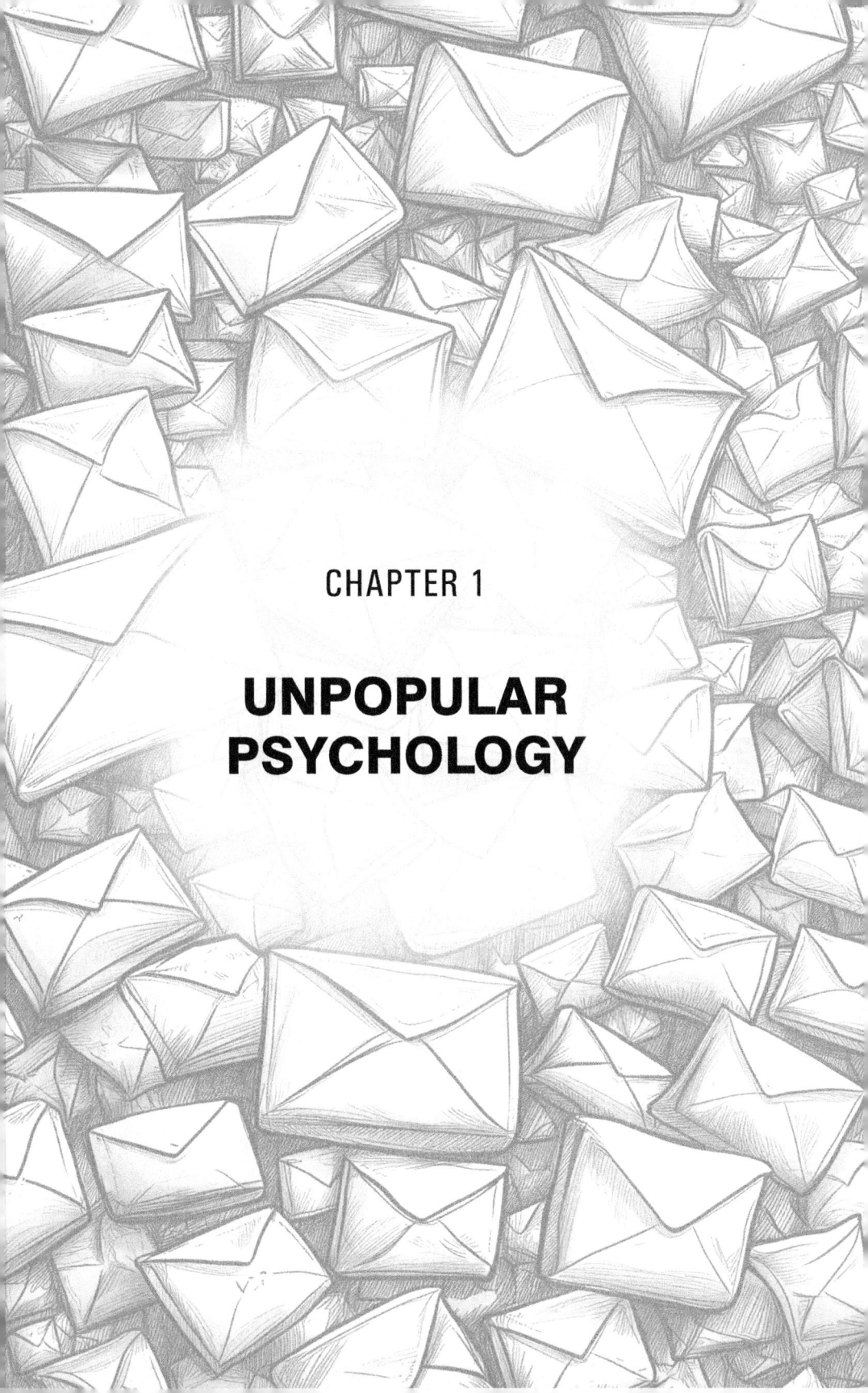

CHAPTER 1

UNPOPULAR PSYCHOLOGY

When trying to read someone's mind there's something you have to remember…

'You can't actually read people's minds.'

What you *can* do is use a mocktail of human psychology, influence, statistical likelihoods, reading non-verbal cues, *and* some quick improvisational thinking.

Before having a total meltdown because I missed home, my family and friends so much, I built a 17-year career as a 'mind reader and comedian'. Companies flew me around the world to entertain their guests and staff with my shows. To keep travelling the world, you have to get good at it.

For 17 years, I honed my craft to the point I was performing for corporations and celebrities. I regularly got asked to teach my techniques to other performers, and ended up writing 10 books about said techniques.

I lectured at The Magic Circle in London and was invited to The Magic Castle in Hollywood. I helped out and advised on stage shows and TV shows for magicians. I filmed a TV pilot with Uri Geller, and was on a BBC TV show exposing fraudulent psychics.

I got to do a lot of cool things. And *learn* a lot of cool things.

The thing that's always struck me is, when using psychology, if you lose the sale, you move on to the next prospect.

And for me? If I didn't get it right on stage, in front of thousands of people...I wouldn't have a career. This stuff *has* to work.

My techniques needed to be reliable so I could confidently get the result - night after night, wherever I was in the world, whoever I'd speak to.

An Outsider's Curiosity, The Birth of a Business

Human psychology has always fascinated me.

It probably comes from being an outsider as a kid.
Never the popular one.
Didn't like sports.
Very fussy eater.
Young Kennedy just wanted to figure out how to be liked.

I remember reading *How to Win Friends and Influence People* in high school.

Poor lad. I wish Young Kennedy had just relaxed more. Accepted himself, y'know?

Luckily, this fascination for psychology and the human mind turned into a really successful career, where I've now performed across the UK, USA, Asia, and I've even been to Antarctica!

(Fucking freezing by the way. Beautiful. But freezing.)

Because of this success, other entertainers then started asking me about how I built such a successful business.

How was I so booked up?

How was I getting paid so much money for these gigs?

In the end, I created a small 'side business' that I ran from hotel rooms and departure lounges between gigs[1], where I helped other entertainers book more gigs, increase their prices, and earn more money.

It started as an email course called *Gig Flow*, where people received an email-a-day each with the next step to take, building a system day by day. After a few months, people told me they wanted more, so I expanded it into a full membership program with a monthly physical print newsletter.

Digital courses online, a physical print newsletter, emails...I had it all going on! And through the very

---

1   This totally makes me sound like a pimp.

tools I'll be teaching you in this book, I grew that little *side hustle* into a nice six-figure business.

And that's all down to the power of email.

Email Marketing - You Beautiful Bastard!

I had my email list in AWeber, (one of the OGs of email marketing service providers). Loved it. It felt like magic! I could merge someone's name into an email automatically, making it feel personal.

These were amazing times. I emailed every day, promoting the magic tricks I'd invented, my books, courses, and membership. I'd tell stories, give tips… all leading to an offer.

I loved that from anywhere in the world, I could write an email, and it would make me money. Using email turned my little laptop into an ATM- it legit felt like cheating!

I started applying this email stuff to the gigs side of things. I even created an automated email sequence that followed up once someone booked me, offering them what we'd call an up-sell–an additional special thing I could do for their event (and they could pay me an extra $2,500 for it).

This was when I started realising how much I love email marketing.

With my email list, I could do anything:

- If I was speaking at an event, I could fill the room up by dropping an email.
- If I was being interviewed on a podcast, I could drive listeners with an email.
- If I wanted to know what to sell next, I'd just ask what people wanted by...sending an email.

I realised that owning a list of people who like your topic–and being able to send a message right to them–is the most powerful thing in the world.

With this, I'd never struggle for money, I'd never struggle for connection, I'd never struggle for a way to get my voice heard.

Later, after losing all of my savings in a tech startup (another story for another time), I got asked by other businesses to talk about what I was doing with email marketing.

And it turns out not only am I really good at it, but I love talking about it, too!

Since then, I've been the CEO of Email Marketing

Heroes, and I've helped more than 8,000 businesses make more money from their emails.

That's not to mention the hundreds of thousands of people I've helped for free through:

- My long-running free podcast and YouTube channel, *The Email Marketing Show*
- Keynotes at events worldwide
- My online courses and memberships
- Guest podcasts I've been interviewed on
- Training sessions for various business groups

And now...I'm doing it in this book, too.

Now that you know the unusual perspective I bring to all of this stuff, shall we bloody well get into the actionable *how-to*?

The free resources I've put together for this book are more than you get in most $1,997 products.

Get them by scanning the QR code with your phone camera:

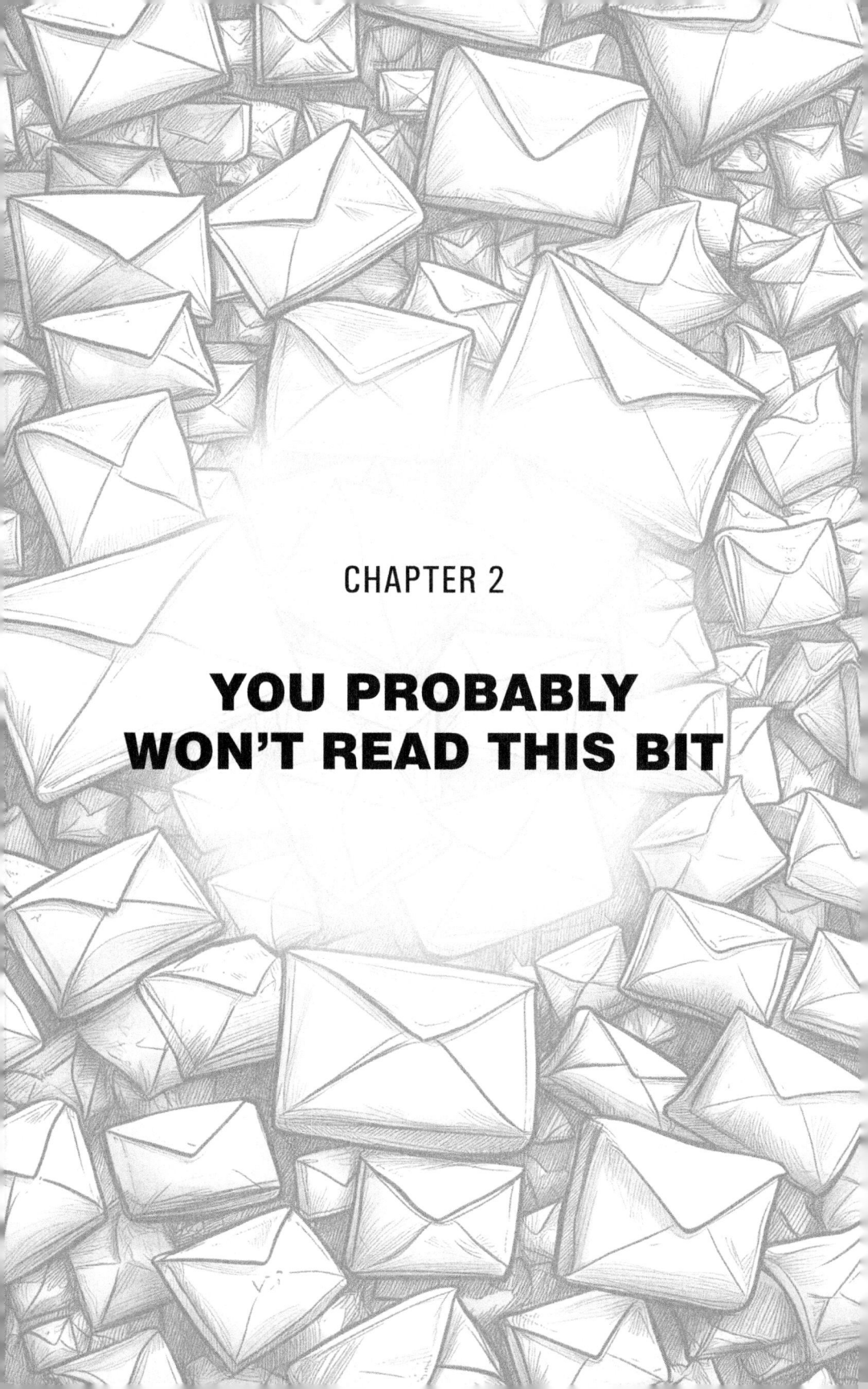

CHAPTER 2

YOU PROBABLY WON'T READ THIS BIT

First off, I'm writing this myself.

No AI going on here. No ghostwriter, either. (Luckily, for your sake I *do* have an editor to cut out my over use of commas).

I'm (bitterly) sitting here on my sofa in my dressing gown, suffering from vomit-inducing vertigo, channelling my thoughts to you through this laptop. It's the only thing keeping me distracted from feeling like I'm living on a fairground waltzer.

Let's get into it...

The Reality of Email Marketing Costs

When you grow your email list, you do it to make money by serving those people. Whether it's with tips on running their business, mindset shifts, or whatever it is you promised them when they signed up for your wisdom.

That's how it works.

It's just like the orange, tan-encrusted business speaker Zig Ziglar (the inspiration behind the Spice Girls' 'a zig a zig ah'[2]) said: "*You can have everything in life you want, if you will just help other people get what they want*".

---

2 Not really.

But, here's the thing-each year, the cost of running your business goes up. Even with email marketing, which has little to no overhead to speak of, the cost of getting people onto your email list can only go up.

On the Meta platforms, the cost of 1,000 impressions has rocketed 61% year on year. And Google's impressions are up 75% year on year, according to Business Insider. You may also notice the cost of the software to run your business is also increasing (because the costs of those businesses creating said software are also rising).

Even the cost of running your life keeps going up. (How much is a bloody bar of chocolate now? I remember when it was 30p. Now I sound like my grandma.)

What I'm getting at is, you get fewer subscribers for the same amount of money.

That's why I urgently put together this book. So you can have a playbook to grow your business no matter how much it costs to get a lead or subscriber. While your competitors are flapping about trying to figure out both lead acquisition *and* then how to convert those new leads, you'll be making money from your new subscribers.

This isn't theory. What you have here is a practical playbook based on generating more than $2.6 million in sales in this one business alone. And it's a playbook with proven, tested techniques, that I've shared with over 8,400 of my paying students all around the world.

Some of what you've got here, I've spotlighted in my keynotes on stage at events such as Atomicon, Entrepreneur's Marketing Conference and AdCon where I've shared the stage with the likes of Ryan Deiss, Steven Bartlett, Daniel Priestley, Ali Abdaal and Perry Belcher.

A lot of this, I have only ever shared inside of high-level closed-door masterminds like Todd Brown's Top 1 in Florida and Jon Penberthy's Titan in the UK, each carrying a $35,000 membership fee. And you now have this high level information in your hands.

The reason is simple. It's needed.

Not only is the cost of advertising continuing to rise, but conversion rates are lower as we all get more skeptical of marketing.

Using this system, you'll create a consistent, predictable flow of sales from your email list - a system that will simultaneously solve the list growth problem.

YOU PROBABLY WON'T READ THIS BIT

Fuck Facebook Ads. People paid a $97 for a seat at this training which shows you how to make your business immune to advertising costs.

Yours free, just scan the QR code with your phone camera:

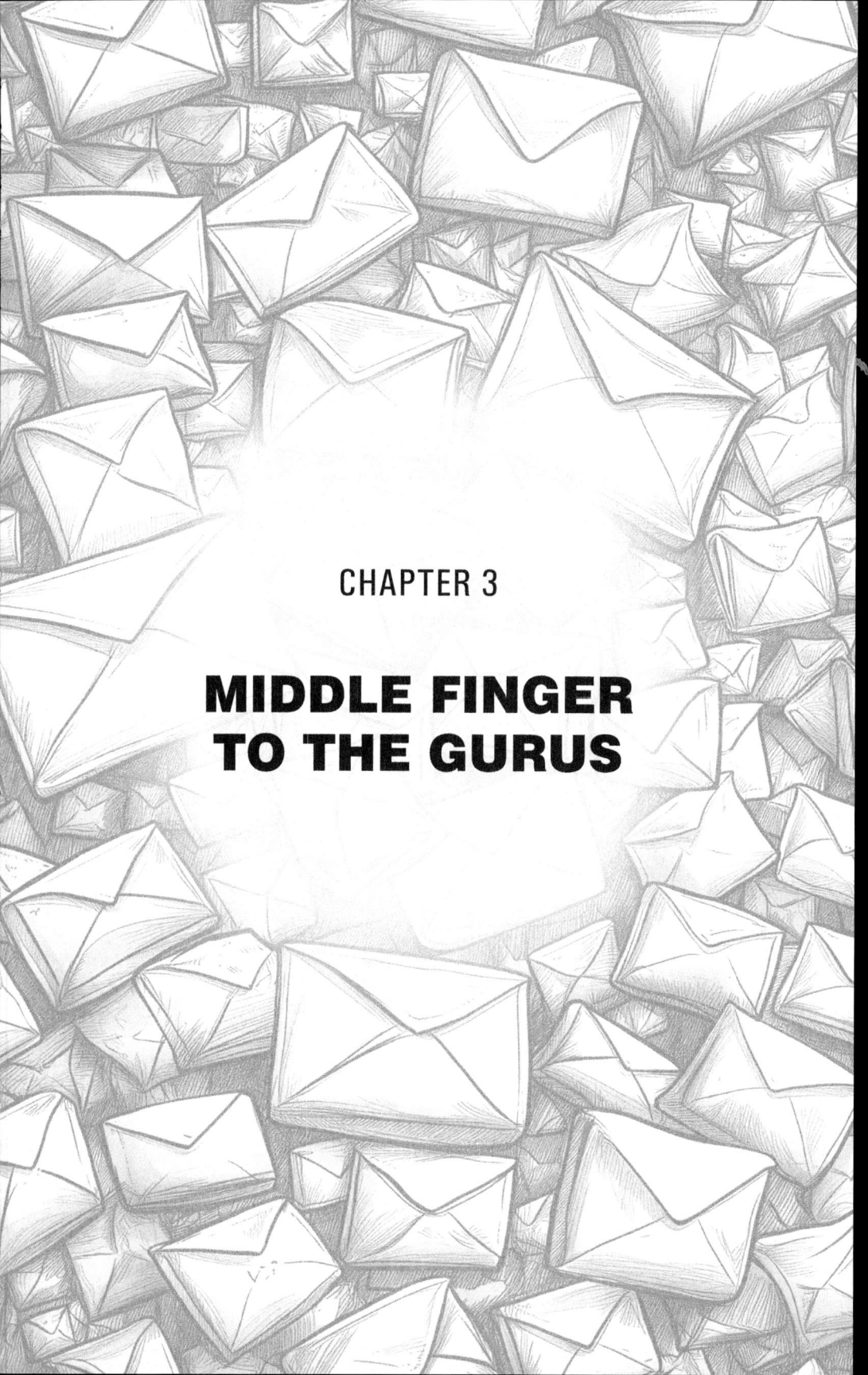

CHAPTER 3

MIDDLE FINGER TO THE GURUS

It was early 2021 and I was on a sales call with one of the biggest names in the online marketing space.

The guy's one of the highest paid copywriters in the world, made a bajillion dollars, worked for some of the biggest names on the planet and is a really, really nice guy.

Successful and nice as hell.

Love him.

And he's telling me how, by having him install his super-duper system, it would get me towards that goal everyone has of making $1 per subscriber per month.

By that, he meant that if we had 10,000 people on our list, we'd be making $10,000 a month from it. ($1 for each subscriber, each month.) And if you do some research, you'll quickly see that's a common goal most people reach for.

What do you think I did?

Well, you're smart, so you probably already realised that I said, 'Fuck, no.'

We were already making between $12 - $30 each month per subscriber, depending on the month and what we were promoting.

So dropping to $1 from even just $12 would have put us out of business within days.

At the time, I kind of thought he was the one who needed *our* system in *his* business.

So yeah, that call didn't go great and I did not sign up to his offer, but it did make me realise how much better my approach was.

What *is* this approach I'm teasing you with?

It's simple.

Let's take, for example, Hillary-Marie from New Jersey. Hillary has an online tap dance membership and certification program. (Yeah, she teaches tap dance on the internet. Amazing, right?) She took one of the email campaign sequences I taught her and sent it out to 790 people.

It was only 4 days long, and she filled up her bank account with $16,000 in sales.

790 people.

$16,000 in sales.

That's more than $20 per subscriber. 20x what the 'average goal' is! (Aka 20x what the guru was pitching me).

Am I saying you'll get those results? I have no idea. Obviously. Everyone gets different results. But the thing is...TWENTY TIMES the average!

Twenty times *more* money in the bank.

How Did I Get This 'Super Power'?

Need.

Yeah, simple, old-fashioned necessity.

Until recently, I've always sold in 'micro-niches'. Small niche markets meant I could never expect to have a whopping big email list. Instead, I had to get good at turning the email subscribers I *did* have, into as much money as possible.

This is how I was able to turn a list of around 5,000 people into over $1 million dollars in the bank. And I did it without feeling like I was squeezing my email subscribers dry.

In this book, I'm going to take you through my complete approach to maximising your sales from email marketing, in a way that strengthens your relationship with your subscribers instead of pushing them away.

I'll tell you now that this flies in the face of most of what we have all been taught about email marketing.

That means as you read this whole thing, you'll have doubts, and you'll wonder how you could apply this to how to do things.

I've also intentionally kept it short, to increase your chances of making it to the end and putting this stuff to work.

As you'll see, I have rewritten the game plan on what email marketing is. And by playing a different game, I get different results.

You'll also notice that this is written to be an enjoyable read. The last thing you want is to wade through another Daniel Kahneman book trying to find the will to live to the end of it.

Like in all of my training and programs, fun makes it easier to learn, because it opens up more connections in your mind and makes it easier to implement.

Ready? Put your hard hat on - because from this point on, your email marketing is Under Construction.

Mind The Gap previously only available to paying clients (around $997/year), this closed doors training shows you exactly how to plug the holes in every funnel to squeeze out more profit every single time.

Scan the QR code with your phone for free access to the whole thing!

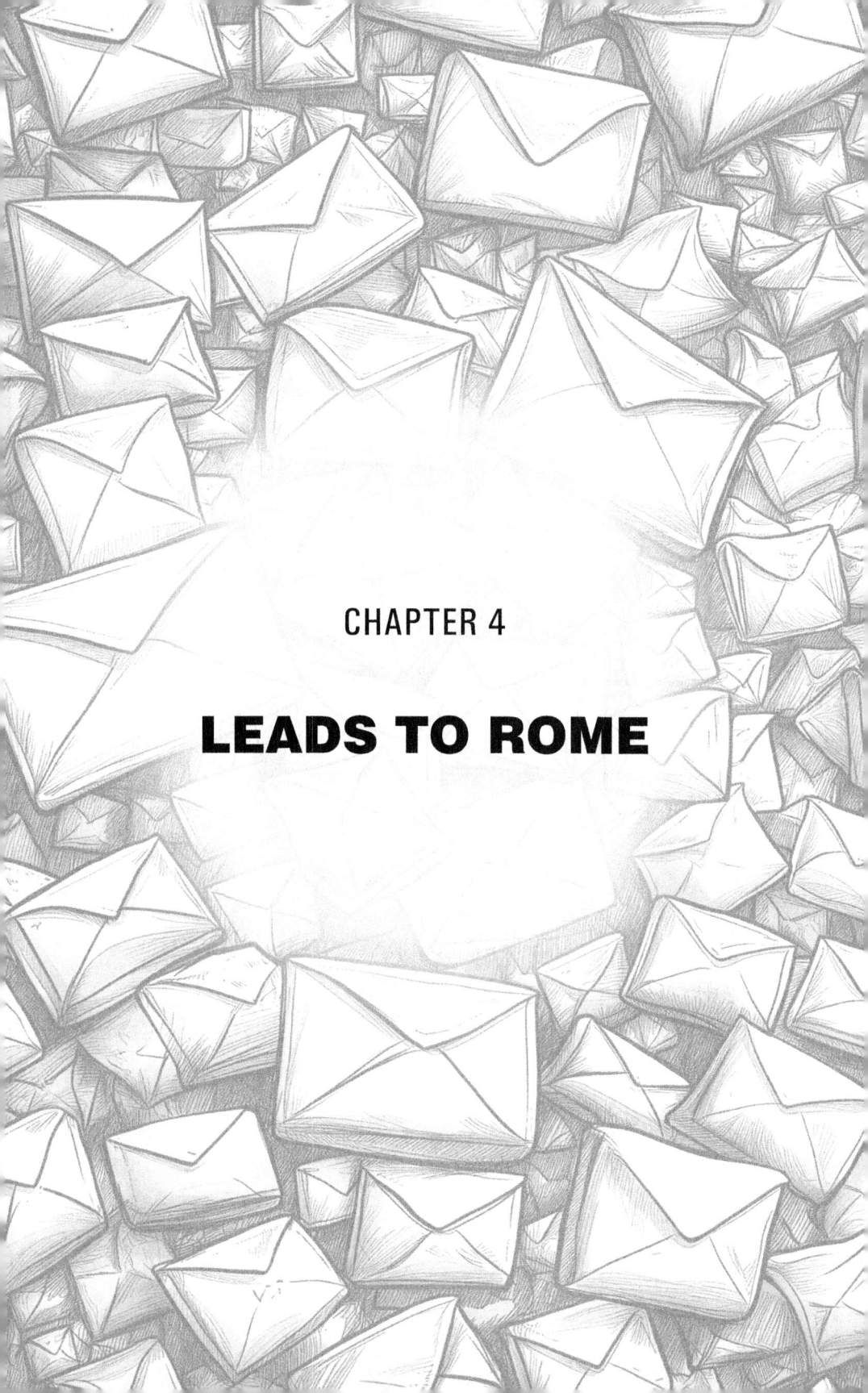

CHAPTER 4

LEADS TO ROME

I'll get to why we were in an underground bank vault in the centre of the financial district of London in a moment, I promise...

It all started when Michelle joined our team to tighten up our operations and help us grow the business. The first thing she did? Review our accounts and Profit & Loss statement.

I've never looked at that. That's our accountant's job– probably something they submit to the government. But, Michelle saw it as the key to understanding our business' financial health.

She immediately asked me the same questions my accountant asked me 2 years ago:

"How are you so profitable? How come you have so much money left over to take home and spend on that hairstyle, after all these expenses of running a business?"

Yes, we have a team, we have ads, we run a podcast and fly around the world to speak and to attend events to learn and grow even more.

But the profit isn't a fluke

And it's no accident, my fine-feathered friend.

The answer is the system you've got in your hands right now. It all boils down to one simple concept, first shared at one of our Mastermind Days... (Which we hosted in a super cool old bank vault in London.)

All Roads Lead to Rome

To scale in such a profitable way, every business needs to define its "Rome Offer"- the core product or service you want everyone to enroll in.

When I work with private clients, this is one of the very first things I get them to do.

For you, it might be a course, a membership, a mastermind, your app, or a service. The key is to choose something with the capacity and pricing to hit your revenue goals. What's the one thing that you want everyone to be in?

In some cases, it is the thing that has really no limit. It's totally scalable. For example, a self-study course. That's what our *Automated Email Engine* is. It's not our most expensive offer, but it has the highest potential because it scales more than our higher ticket programs, which have a cap.

For you, it might be something similar. Or it may be something that, while it does have a capacity limit for some reason, that limit is high enough that when it's full and everyone is paying, you're hitting your financial goals.

Your Rome offer is your centerpiece. Your flagship.

It's not your low-cost front-end offer, and it's not your profit maximizer or mastermind.

With our clients, we use a simple 1-page worksheet to map out their Rome offer and all the ways to funnel people into it. (You can grab your copy of the worksheet at EmailMarketingBook.com/rome-sheet)

Focusing on Your Rome Offer = Maximum Profitability

To make your email list as profitable as possible, we want all roads to lead to your 'Rome Offer'.

No distractions.

Everything you're doing is to lead people ultimately to be in a position to enroll or buy that.

And I mean *everything*.

This book isn't designed to be theoretical. I'm not going to leave you with just the concept, don't worry. Let's show you how we're doing it, m'kay?

Instead of offering a messy catalog of products, which confuses both you and your audience, you simplify.

I'll give you an example. A friend of mine spent six hours trying to buy a new Kindle recently but was paralysed with confusion about the differences between the various models and which one would be best for him. After a couple of weeks, he still had no clue which one to buy, so he called me and just asked which one I bought.

Bewildered subscribers don't buy.

Or do anything useful, in fact.

If your subscribers don't clearly understand what you're offering, they'll freeze. And if you're constantly worrying about what to sell or switching up your offers...you're going to be paralysed and distracted, too.

Think of your Rome Offer as the central hub. Everything you do should direct people towards it.

Take Brad G, for example. His Rome Offer is a membership where he helps Christian musicians get *their music* in front of more people. Ultimately, he wants everyone in that membership.

He used one of our email sequences (just seven emails) and ran it to his existing subscribers on his list.

From that promotion, Brad made $3,700 in sales.

But that wasn't the real win. After each sale, he invited customers to join his membership, turning on-time buyers into recurring revenue. Money hitting his bank account every month.

So yes, he made $3,700, but, most importantly, he grew his Rome Offer, his membership.

All roads lead to Rome.

Putting The Offer Into Practice

Let me take you behind the scenes into our business, for example. For us, *The Automated Email Engine* is *the Rome Offer*. Everything we do is to help people see the value in it, so they'll want to enroll. That's all we obsess over. Different routes, paths and on-ramps to move subscribers into this program.

This makes life simpler for us *and* for our subscribers. Instead of juggling multiple disconnected offers, we create strategic stepping stones that lead people into Email Engine.

For example, we have other mini courses too, like Subject Lines that Make Sales. It looks like a stand alone product, but it's actually a pathway into Email Engine.

And once someone buys our Subject Lines that Make Sales mini course, what do we do? We offer them the chance to upgrade to our full Blueprint.

Later, we might show up saying, "Hey we have this awesome email campaign called the Encore Upsell Campaign - it's just 5 emails that'll jack your sales up…"

We include a video where we show how we and hundreds of our students are switching to this method of using some reverse psychology to make their tripwires and upsells convert even better.

It's a full package. Looks like a new product. Smells like a new product. It has its own sales page describing the whole thing in detail. Selling it.

But no, we did not create a new campaign to sell. It's one of 47 campaigns we already had, repackaged as a stepping stone.

And when we do offer it, some of our subscribers think "Oh damn, I got to have that!" and they buy it.

What's on the next page…?

Yes! An offer to upgrade to our Email Engine program.

Again: all roads lead to Rome.

Why This Works (and What Happens if You Don't Do it)

The alternative is that your subscriber gets emails from you each month with different offers from you. They're all in your wheelhouse of expertise, but they're all *different*. They all lead down different *paths*.

So, what happens in their minds here?

They become distracted.

Their attention–the very thing that, as marketing people who are selling things, we know we need to control and direct - is all over the place.

And if they're distracted, you're not making sales.

Think about it: If you email subscribers about a new product every month, on top of all the other offers they get on a daily basis, how can they possibly understand, like *deeply* understand, what your main offer is? Furthermore, how can they actually feel its value so strongly that they interrupt that bootleg game of Flappy Bird to go and buy it from you?

Answer –they can't.

They have too many things they're trying to understand. And what's more, they're also playing a torturous game of Spot the Bloody Difference between your different offers!

How many times have you heard of a customer being confused between your different offers? You know, thinking this one included 'that thing' but it didn't because it's part of *another* thing. They get in touch to ask: "Is this the same as XYZ Product I already bought?"

That's, sadly, an issue I see all too often. Because even though *you* know they're totally different... Your subscribers aren't blessed with the detailed understanding of your business that you have.

And you've probably dealt with this yourself when you get an email from someone offering their 'new' thing - that new thing that sounds a LOT like the 'old' thing.

I'm sure in the creator's mind, it's a different thing altogether. But from the outside, it's like... "Errrr, what now?"

We made this mistake ourselves. We had a program about writing endless, high-converting emails.

Great promise, right?

But then we launched a separate product about our amazing email campaigns... And all of a sudden, it becomes a case of, "Hang on, what's the difference between the 'unlimited emails' and these campaigns? Surely a campaign is just a string of emails with some time delays between them?"

To us, it was obvious. To our subscribers? Not so much.

It's even tougher for subscribers to really understand what you can help them with when they're also getting emails from all those other marketers they're subscribed to. If your messaging isn't laser-focused, your offer gets drowned in the noise.

The Secret Sauce

This is one of the main reasons that we are able to make so much from our email list: We find different reasons to get people into our Rome offer.

That's the skill we've obsessed over and become the best in the world at.

And it all comes from realising you *have* a Rome offer. Everything you do after, is about moving people closer to it.

You can download our Rome Offer Worksheet at EmailMarketingBook.com/rome-sheet (no cost). That's where your work begins...but it's only the *beginning*.

Because in theory, the Rome Offer alone is perfect to engage your subscribers. But what happens when those subscribers have lost interest *before they even hear* about your Rome offer?

And it happens all the time. You see your email open rates dropping. And that clickthrough rate is so sad, it could be an Adele song.

No one wants that.

Next, we're going to get into fixing this...

ACTION:

Decide on your Rome Offer. What is it you're building your business around? This will give you direction for all of your marketing decisions. Write down your Rome offer and start looking at how everything else is either a lead IN to it, or a profit maximiser FROM it. The Rome of the Hub that links everything.

Rome Offer 1-Pager. Nail the right Rome offer that will serve you.

Download the Rome Offer 1-Pager by scanning the QR code:

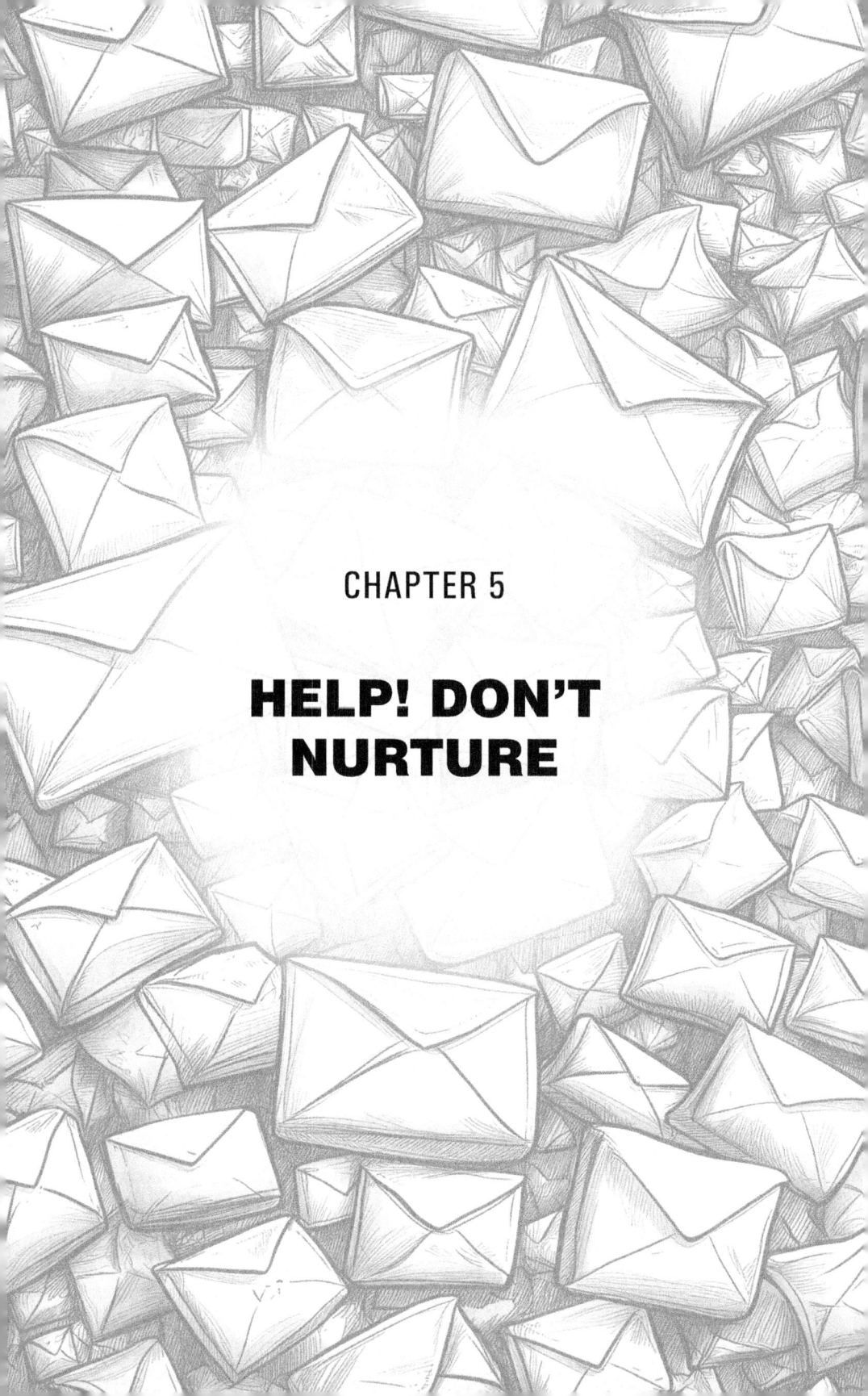

CHAPTER 5

HELP! DON'T NURTURE

You've had a horrible accident.

Your leg is hanging off, and there's blood spurting all over the place.

You rush to the hospital. (Or hop to the hop-ital - that's a Dad joke for you; you're welcome). Your friends and family gather around with flowers. (And grapes, for some reason[3]).

In the emergency room, a doctor comes rushing over, looks at your plight and begins with, "Let me tell you why I came into the medical profession. I was born in 1984 and my parents were both doctors and..."

You've hit the floor, out cold before he can finish. The blood loss got you.

This ridiculous story illustrates that when people join your email list, some of them have a problem–a gap in their life, a need, or a want–that is urgent for them to solve *right now*. They're not joining your list to get more emails in their inbox or just because you're sexy.

And this is where so much of the email marketing advice we've been given lets our subscribers bleed

---

[3] Why grapes? Every time someone's in hospital 'oh better go get them some grapes'. Are they the miracle cure doctors aren't telling us about? Does anyone even eat grapes in everyday life?

out. So, let's take a deeper look at the psychology and mindset of these folks who join your email list.

The Mindset You Need to Understand

Everyone who subscribes to your newsletter gets on there through a lead magnet ("Hey, get this free thing–the price is your email address"), a newsletter sign up, or by buying something from you. If we were to segment it, it would look like this:

HOW PEOPLE END UP ON YOUR LIST	WHY THEY END UP ON YOUR LIST
Free Lead Magnet	Learn
Signed Up for Newsletter	Fix/Solve
Bought Something from You	Improve

We also know that they think you might have a solution.

Some of these people want that solution right now. Or yesterday, ideally. But if you don't sell time machines, then *right now* will have to do.

I'm sure I'm not the only person who's joined email lists just to find out what they have for sale, so I can buy the help that I need.

Buuuuut....

We've all been taught to nurture people.

"Let them know your origin story, your hero's journey, why you do what you do, build credibility and then start building desire. Give them value and build up 'good will' so they'll buy something."

Problem is, by the time you do all that, your buyers have bled out.

And by 'bled out,' I mean they went somewhere else and bought the answer from someone else.

They handed your money to someone else who wasn't getting in their own way. And by someone else, I mean your competitors–who probably have a solution that's not as good as yours.

Shame.

People don't buy stuff because you sent them some lovely articles for a while and eventually they felt indebted to you. They buy stuff from you because it'll solve an active problem in their life.

Don't Nurture, Deliver The Solution

Ashley, a magician from the UK, is a perfect example of delivering the solution and striking while the iron is hot. He started helping other performers to book more gigs. Instead of nurturing them to death, he knew his magicians have a real pain point–they're desperate for better paying gig bookings.

Now, this is a small niche. His list was only 35 people.

But that's still 35 people who need help.

So Ashley ran one of our super-short campaigns that lasted just 72 hours and raked in £13,000 British pounds (that's about $16,000 USD).

In 72 hours. From 35 people.

By helping them, instead of nurturing them.

I've joined so many email lists and for the first few days, I've learned loads of stuff I just don't care about. And what happened? It caused me to do something worse than not buy, it caused me to lose interest.

It meant that I stopped paying attention. I stopped opening that person's emails.

I became a lurker.

A lurker who they paid to get on their email list. But someone who wouldn't buy, because I got trained to be uninterested.

YOU trained me to be uninterested. *You.*

And that's a punch in the gut.

We're all creatures of behavioural patterns. So let's not train someone into being bored when they see our name drop in their email inbox. Let's instead train them to expect solutions, things that will serve our businesses and themselves. Solutions that are worth *investing* in.

Training Subscribers For Action

Training people that we sell things is important early on in their relationship with them.

Hey, if you went on a date and the person is into weird kinky shit, you'd want to know that before you've spent too much on dates and bought a house together. Right?

The perfect way to do this is to just mention a paid product inside your very first email in your welcome sequence.

Our 'Welcome Sequence' (the first set of emails a subscriber gets from us) is called the "Getting To Know You" sequence (more on that later) and, at four emails long, it's the only "nurturing" we do for new subscribers before getting straight to sales.

Even in our welcome email, there's a link right to our flagship Automated Email Engine offer, for those who want to jump in straight away.

But, critically, it's not about us, our hero's journey etc. It's about the things our subscribers care about:

- Them.
- Their problem.
- How we're going to solve it in a new way.

Here's the thing: Most people are nurturing their email subscribers to death.

There are people who need a solution, have the cash held high in the air, and want to buy.

We're always trained to believe that we have to *sell, sell, sell...* forgetting that there is a segment of your audience who are ready to *buy, buy, buy*. They don't need romancing to buy from you.

And we need to prioritise them first, before they run off with someone else.

That's why, right after your "Getting to Know You" sequence, you need a direct sales sequence that sells the solution.

Don't put off the urgent buyer for fear of upsetting the people who need more time.

They'll be okay; they'll get time.

By leading with a paid offer your first emails, you'll see those urgent buyers stepping up to buy. And those early sales really help with cash flowing ad costs.

ACTION:

From this section, I really want you to stop nurturing your subscribers to death. With every email you send, you're either bringing them closer to you or you're adding more distractions and overwhelm, which pushes them away. Make an offer in the first emails as soon as people join, and the people ready to jump in will do so.

HELP! DON'T NURTURE

Conversion Ready Offer - The best emails in the world can't convert an offer that's not primed for conversion by email. In this training I show you the step by step process for making sure your offer is conversion optimised. This is not some generic method or checklist, this is a system to test your offer to your audience.

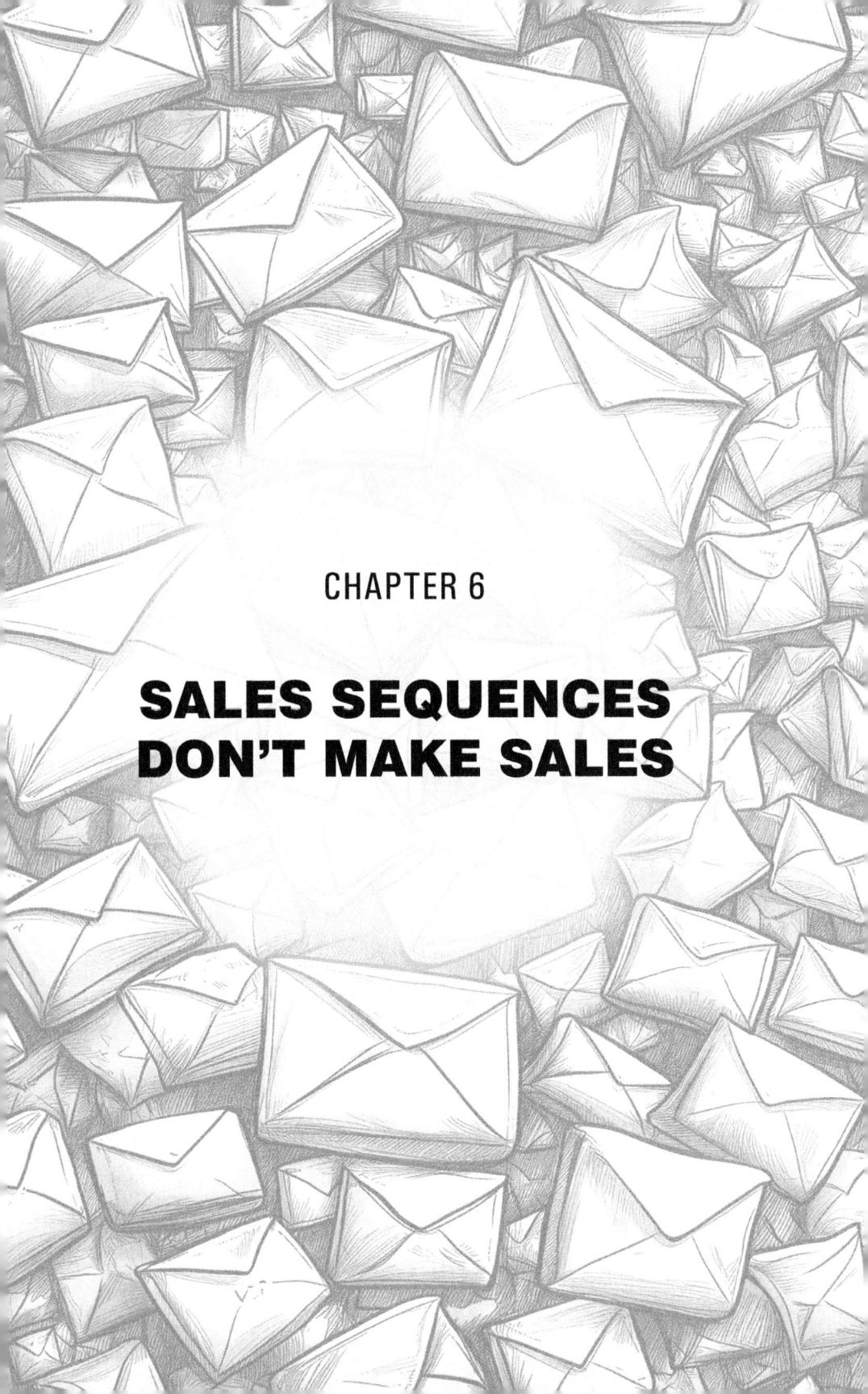

CHAPTER 6

SALES SEQUENCES DON'T MAKE SALES

I wanted to know how to run one of those online challenges. You know, those free 5-day events that are essentially Jeff Walker's Product Launch Formula but dressed up in fancy new clothes.

I wanted the details. I'm a 'details' person.

Luckily for me, some chap was advertising his lead magnet, promising to show me how exactly to do it.

So, I'm opting in.

And I'm refreshing my inbox like any self-respecting ADHD marketer.

Finally an email from him. Subject line:

Bonus #2 Expires Tonight!

Oh...?

Where's my free report?

What *is* Bonus 2?

What was Bonus 1?

Hang on...what's the fucking PRODUCT?!

I had so many questions.

Being so confused, you can imagine, this paralysed

me from buying. Or from ever engaging in this guy's stuff at all, really.

It was like I was back at school, seeing the other kids giggling and whispering while I stood on the outside, excluded from the conversation.

No, I wasn't the coolest kid at school. I wasn't bullied or anything serious like that. I was always just...an outsider.

The Importance of a Sales Sequence

You don't want your new subscribers to feel like outsiders either.

When people join our email lists, all it takes is a simple six-day email sequence that introduces your product or service.

This goes right after the welcome sequence. We call it a sales campaign.

Without one, your subscribers won't have the context they need for your offer.

How many times have you joined someone's list, only to start receiving whatever emails they happen to be sending, with *no* real idea about what they're selling?

When this happens, our readers have to work far too hard to understand the offer. Before they can even decide whether they *want* it, they're already overwhelmed.

It doesn't matter how big a discount you give or how impressive your testimonials are - if they don't know what the product or service is, it's impossible for someone to make the decision to buy.

Context + Offer legitimisation

We need a campaign of emails that properly and fully introduces our Rome Offer - our core product or service.

But it's more than just sending a few emails.

To illustrate, let me tell you about April.

April has a wonderful business, helping struggling and dyslexic readers. After years of working with us, she's grown from nearly quitting (joining us was her giving it 'one last chance') to now running a 7-figure business that changes lives.

I get emotional pretty much every time I speak with April because the work she's doing is giving people the gift of being able to read.

Imagine that. A life without having been able to read and then, one day, it's all opened up to you. Amazing stuff.

April had things set up so everyone who joined her email list first went through our Getting to Know You welcome sequence and then straight into a sales sequence, just like what we've been speaking about here. (April is obviously a super smart woman. Although she'll tell you she's "just a grandma who came up with this system".)

After that sequence, subscribers entered another sequence where they were offered an additional bonus to join her Rome Offer.

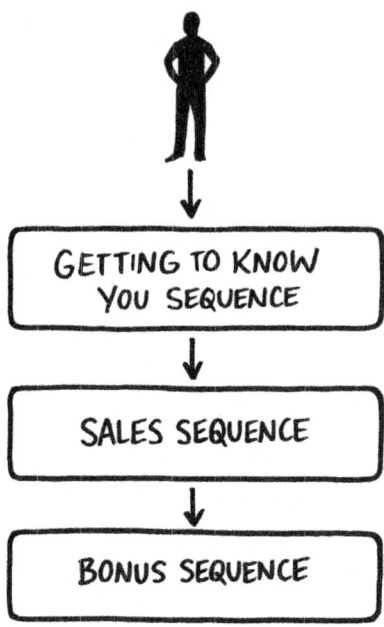

That 'extra bonus' campaign converted like crazy. Rocking it every day. Making sales. Beautiful.

But her sales sequence? Not so much.

Naturally, she considered ditching the sales campaign and jumping straight from the welcome sequence into this 'extra bonus' campaign.

Until I waved my hands in the air and begged her not to.

Why Keep The Sales Campaign?

Let's leave your creative entrepreneur mind thinking about that for just one moment, shall we?

The sales sequence before wasn't working.

So...why *wouldn't* she throw it out?

The answer: Context + Offer Legitimisation.

(Damn, I wish someone had talked to me about this years ago when I was starting.)

Imagine this: I don't know about where you live, but here in the North East of England, we have these furniture shops that sell sofas and constantly advertise on TV their latest sale. "20% off all items– ends Monday!"

SALES SEQUENCES DON'T MAKE SALES

And...they say the same thing every week.

We ran a poll on our @emailmarketingheroes Instagram recently to ask our followers what they think when they see those ads. The response was incredible.

Everything from 'Yeah, and then another one starts next week' to flat out calling BS on them.

This is happening because there is no *offer legitimacy*.

If you've never seen the product at full price, a discount doesn't feel like a real deal–it just feels like the price. (We're talking about the general public here. Skeptical as hell about discounts.)

The same happens with your email list. If the first thing they see about your offer is a discount or a bonus, they have no frame of reference. They don't know what the product usually costs or includes.

"Is this really a discount? Or is this just another false claim on the Internet?"

Having the full price, regular offer before the 'extra bonus thing' makes that extra bonus thing real. Your subscribers see the full price and understand the product's value before any discounts or bonuses come into play. (That's why April's bonus offer was doing so spectacularly–*because* of the sales sequence she had in place.)

And when you add a bonus later, it's clear that it's an *extra*. It's special.

And it works.

Of course, that's assuming you can hold your subscribers' attention long enough for them to read your sales sequence–and take action. But how do we do that in a world where everyone is blind to the bigger and bigger promises and more outrageous claims that none of us believe any more? We're fixing that next!

ACTION:
Put a sales campaign into your automations so that every person who joins your list is fully introduced to your Rome Offer. You'll see sales from your other campaigns jump up too because your audience now has context, and your offer is legitimised.

Proving and Being Believed is harder today than ever. I have a whole playbook of techniques I use to build trust and let someone see what I am saying is true - even when it's something unbelievable (usually because the results are crazy or they're in a hyper skeptical market). You have access to this using the QR code:

CHAPTER 7

GRANDMOTHER'S FALSE TEETH

The words we say can be interpreted in different ways. They can be believed and they can be ignored. But there is something much more important than the words. Let me show you...

When I was in acting school, there was this exercise where you'd say the same phrase, but with emphasis on a different word each time.

It gets bloody funny.

But it starts off with the emphasis on the very first word: *__I__* didn't steal your grandmother's false teeth.

What do we take from that? The false teeth have been stolen, but it wasn't me. Simple.

Shift the emphasis to the word 'steal' and it becomes: I didn't *__steal__* your grandmother's false teeth.

So, you...borrowed them?

And that's not even the most ridiculous one:

I didn't steal your grandmother's *__false__* teeth.

Funny!

This exercise taught me that words themselves are a *tiny* part of meaning, emotion, and storytelling. The same words, that same 'script' or 'copy', can be said in no less than six different ways, to create completely different meanings–from denying a crime to perhaps assaulting an old woman.

Very different outcomes.

And you know yourself that the words 'I'm fine!' when spoken by your partner can mean things *are* fine or, conversely, that things are very much *not* fine.

Why This Matters in Email Marketing

With this in mind, it's extra surprising that so many people who teach email marketing focus only on *writing* better emails. They focus on the right words to snag people's attention, get them emotionally aroused, and then use psychology to 'put the whammy on them'.

That's the *copywriting* approach.

Of course, it makes sense–emails *are*, after all, made up of words.

And that's why if you look around, you see that everyone else who's teaching email marketing is a *copywriter*.

They're students of writing persuasive language. They're masters of NLP (Neuro Linguistic Programming), persuasion techniques, embedded commands, and psychological subterfuge. Stuffing Prof Robert Cialdini's principles into their emails left, right, and centre.

But, here's the thing: I'm not a copywriter.

In fact I *hire copywriters* to write sales pages and videos when I can.

Sure, I know about psychology. But anyone who's studied communication skills or psychology knows that the words themselves make up a tiny percentage of what we understand when someone says something.

The rest? It's all about *how* it's said and the *context* it's said in.

And this is the <u>*huuuuuge*</u> thing.

The Big Mistake Most Email Marketers Make

Since everyone else teaching email marketing comes from a copywriting background, they focus heavily on wordsmithing–the thing that actually makes the *smallest* impact.

But as I illustrated earlier, those words can have their meaning completely changed by:

- Context
- Emphasis
- Repetition
- Strategy

Meanwhile, over here? My students and I are tapping into *everything else* that moves the needle when it comes to impact.

While everyone else is trying to breed faster horses (write better copy), we're building the motorcar.

We're playing a different game–one that's not focused on the words themselves or trying to *wordsmith* our way into a sale, but on strategic campaign structures that make sales happen

When Words Aren't Enough, You Need a Strategy

This is how we're able to smash through the $1 per subscriber per month that the 'copy-focused' gurus aim for. We're tapping into the strategy that allows us to earn $12 - $30 for every subscriber.

A healthy, well-bred Quarter Horse can reach top speeds of 55 mph, whereas a 2021 Mercedes-AMG GT hits over 200 mph. (Yes, I had to look that up because I know *nothing* about cars. I've never passed my driving test. Control freak issues–a story for another day.)

But my point is this: Faster **horses will never beat a car.**

Cripes, would you even *want* to ride a horse doing 200 mph? Or even 100? You'd need to strap on that Stetson.

The reason most people's emails under-perform is simple: they're trying to wordsmith their way into a sale.

They're fighting with words.

They're racing with horses.

But these days, we're all so bombarded with marketing copy–promises, sales tactics, and gimmicks–that our levels of skepticism are higher than ever.

And now that A.I. can churn out copy in minutes, email content has become commoditised.

Words alone are no longer enough.

Knowing what to say to hook attention doesn't work if you've already *lost* your audience's attention or trained them to tune you out.

Even the most perfectly formed call to action (CTA) means fuck all if no one opens your emails, if they've been let down before, or they've become blind to your repetitive sales tactics.

(Did someone say you're running *another* discount... *puhlease!*)

The Secret to Breaking Through

This isn't to make anyone feel bad. Instead, it's to show you why what you're doing has a limited ceiling on what it can do for you. And probably why it feels like it's harder than others make it appear–and why so many people feel like they need to spend so much time and money on building a mahoosive email list.

Seriously, this is such a different approach and it's the reason so many pro copywriters come to me for my campaigns. They know the words. But almost no one understands the *rest* of what truly drives sales through email. It's the reason one of the biggest email copy agencies in the world hire me to be their secret 'man behind the curtain' and advise them on the email strategy for their clients.

The beauty of playing *this* game (instead of the words one) is that you don't even have to be great at writing.

I regularly send emails that are riddled with typos, yet they bring in sales because *what* I am saying and the structures are so powerful. An email you send with typos in is always going to bring in more sales than an email left in *draft* because you're worried about your spelling.

> **Action:**
> **Let go of obsessing over the words and become a student of strategic promotional campaigns. These are the big levers that create serious online sales.**

The Buyer Triggers. There are 5 major Buyer Triggers that cause different people to buy different things. When you use all 5 of them you stack up sales (we multiplied ours by 18x, for example). I've put together a training on those Buyer Triggers for you, just scan the QR code with your phone:

emailmarketingheroes now

The moment your subscribers can predict you, you've lost them.

Keep surprising them, making them feel like 'wow, I can't believe they just did that'.

This resets attention and keeps people coming back.

They use this in TV shows all the time. It's powerful.

Let's go behind the scenes in our business some more, because as you're about to see, I learn a lot from the fuck ups we make.

Splintering Offers

One of the ways we would get people into our membership program was to take an email campaign from inside the membership and make it available for people to buy as a stand-alone product, outside of the membership.

We call this 'splintering'.

You take a piece of your main product, and offer it separately so people can buy a little taster.

This appeals to all those people who didn't want the commitment of an ongoing membership. It also works really well for a higher priced course for those folks who don't want to make such a hefty financial commitment.

Of course, once they've seen how good your splinter item is, they're keen as chips to enroll in the main offer.

Anyway, that's a side-quest lesson. Back to what this chapter is *actually* about–which is even more important.

When Splintering Works

Since our membership was packed with more than 40 different email campaigns, it's easy to take a different campaign each month and make it available as a stand-alone product.

A new splinter every month.

But it has to be a high-value package. So we included:

- ✓ The full email sequence in a Google Doc ready to copy and send.

- ✓ A Campaign Map which shows you how to set it up and how it all works visually.

- ✓ An hour-long detailed video walkthrough of every email in the campaign, unpacking the psychology, structure, strategy, and even the copy.

An awesome package.

And we mailed it to our email subscribers.

Within minutes, Stripe notifications were piling in. People buying the Black Friday campaign. Yes! And 60% of them were upgrading to the full Rome Offer - aka, joining the membership. Yes, yes!

That's sales *today* from people buying the single campaign, *and* recurring income every month their membership renewed.

It was a resounding success.

So we did it again the following month.

This time, the campaign was called 'The Curious Cat'.

This one had great appeal because it's our reverse-psychology method for getting free lead-magnet subscribers to take it upon themselves to start buying from you, quickly.

It's a sexy topic, right? It solves a big problem we all have–getting free subscribers to buy. Of course, we explained it much better and more drool-worthy than that in the sales materials.

So…

New email campaign. New video. New page. New details. New product in our shopping cart.

And in came the sales. It made around 80% as much as the previous one.

The following month, we splintered out our Webinar campaign. We told the story of Brad from Johannesburg, South Africa, who had been crushing it with a live webinar he had been doing every week teaching people how to improve their run marathons.

While most people see a dip in sales when they switch from live to evergreen webinars, Brad saw a boost. His sales increased and he was banking $shit-tons.

But the sales limped in.

Our magic had worn off.

When Boredom Wins…

Why the dip in sales, you ask?

Because we went to people who had bought our previous one-time packages and asked them why they didn't grab the recent ones too.

The novelty had worn off. It was formulaic.

The pages looked the same, the emails followed the same structure. It wasn't novel enough to get their attention any more.

The copywriting couldn't save us. Better, fresher words weren't cutting through.

But, let's not be doom and gloom about this. This made thousands of dollars and was a roaring success. Initially. Sure, it tapered off to a point of not being worth the effort. What was the fix, then?

To get people's attention, we have to interrupt the pattern. We need to do something novel, to make it interesting.

But, showing up with the same format in the same order to those same people each time is going to create sameness.

Let's be clear, I'm not talking about the same words, but the same *formula*, the same *sequence*. The same 'campaign'.

Emails leading to a landing page with a video on, similar price, similar deliverables. That structure, each and every single time.

Yes, we tried to be efficient. We tried to 'do more of what is working' as we've been taught. Or to put it another way, you might just call it *lazy*.

We got lazy.

Yes, you'll have some new people on your list seeing all of this for the first time. But the folks who have been on that list for a few iterations of it are going to have the 'here we go again' feeling. Just like we do when we see the furniture shop advertising *another* sale event.

And that feeling craps all over any curiosity they might have about *what* is inside the offer that's different this time.

Even if there are differences in the product or service, different bonuses, different positioning, you add something in, take something out, in out, in out, shake it all about - if the campaign itself is the same, your subscriber doesn't get as far as checking out the exciting new stuff.

They've already checked *out*.

Shake It Up

And that's why we have three different ways of doing a 'flash sale':

- Our Black Friday campaign (spoiler: it doesn't just work for Black Friday)

- Our Paparazzi Flash Sale
- Our Super Flash Sale.

They are completely unrecognisable from each other in every way. That means they get attention and they get results.

Think about it like you're jiggling the mouse cursor in the minds of your subscribers so they don't go into screensaver mode.

Like when our client Cody brought in $7,713 using our Super Flash Sale campaign from a list of just 3,800 engaged people. He earned $2 per subscriber, (double that crummy $1 per subscriber average) in those six days.

Why? Because he jiggled their mouse (oooerrr!). He used the campaign structure that grabs attention and whips people into a buying frenzy.

It wasn't the same old, same old.

But I didn't realise until around five years ago...

Most people find it difficult to come up with unique campaigns time and time again. For some reason, I find it easy AND fun.

There are two main ways we can make something fresh and exciting. (*This is not dating advice* :P)

Change The Campaign Structure

The first is what we just talked about: having different campaign structures.

- **Change the number of emails.** Maybe your last campaign was 6 emails and you make this one 10 emails.

- **Change the email frequency.** Last time you sent an email every day and then two emails on the last day. So next time, you do two emails on the first day, one every day, and three on the last day

- **Change the medium.** Perhaps last time you sent emails that linked people to watch a video; next time, you could send them to a survey or to register for a webinar, or an interview you gave.

- **Change the 'Big Idea' of the campaign.** Maybe it's a twenty-four-hour discount one time; the next time, you're sending them a survey; the time after that, it's a coupon code or a video about a bonus they can get...

Every part of this looks and feels completely different and so stands out in your subscribers' minds.

In the next chapter, I'll share with you the second strategy. This technique makes writing winning email campaigns way easier and faster - and means you don't have to be a better writer.

> **ACTION:**
>
> **Use a different email campaign for each promotion you do so you can reset your audience's attention, get maximum engagement, and drive sales.**

Cure Click Blindness. A fast way to get more sales is to get more clicks - but if people go 'blind' to the links in your emails, they scroll past, keep reading but never click...*they're no closer to buying*. I have 16 ways I present the call to action in emails that pop off the page and get even the most jaded people clicking to sales pages. Download my personal playbook of 'Click Tricks' using the QR code:

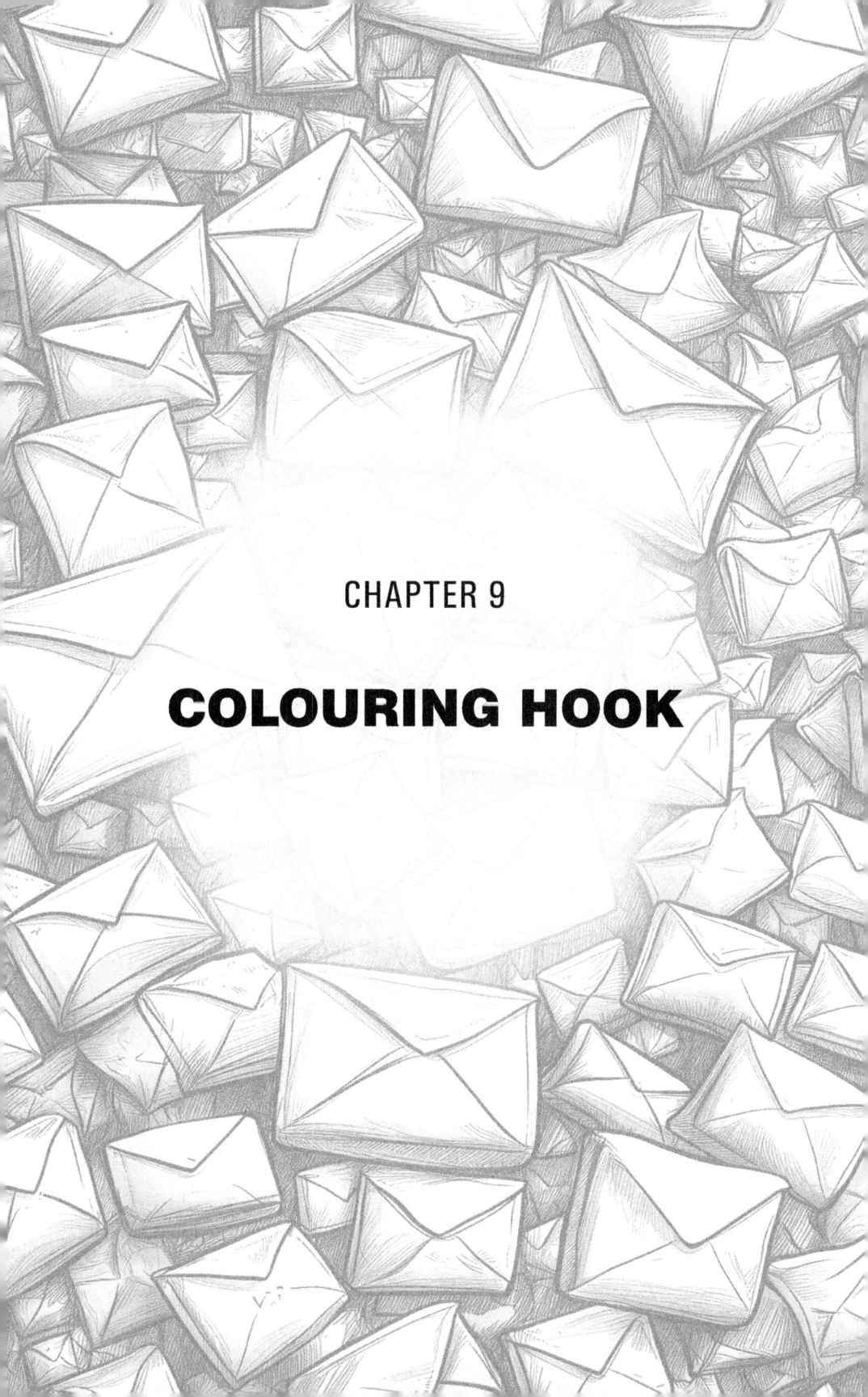

CHAPTER 9

COLOURING HOOK

It's easier to make good-looking pictures if you're just colouring in, right?

Yes, you can still fuck it up, but you'll know it's supposed to be a cat - even if it *has* green paws.

Take my niece and nephew, for example.

Kacie's colouring in. No matter how badly she does it, I can see it's a sheep. A blue-wooled, yellow-eyed demon sheep...but still a sheep.

Whatever the hell young Tommy has drawn, I'm just

going to have to take his word for it. He says it's his mam, but it could be a fence.

The difference? Kacie is just colouring in. Tommy is drawing on a blank sheet of paper.

Frameworks

One of *the* hardest things about writing emails is that blank page.

That's why I never start with a blank page.

Before I write a single word, I write the hook for each email in the campaign.

The Hook is the main message, the *one thing* that email has to do or say.

- For a single, stand-alone email, I'll decide on its hook before writing it.
- For a campaign sequence of emails, I write out all of the hooks first.

The hooks are the outlines in the colouring book.

Even if you don't have the best copywriting skills in the world, as long as you hit that hook, your email will communicate that message.

For example, the first email of one of our campaigns might be: 'A Quick Announcement'.

That's the outline on the page of the colouring book. So now, the email you write would probably be something that quickly announces your new offer. It would be short, snappy, and drive people to check out the sales or registration page.

Another example could be: 'There's a Lot of Work Involved'.

In this email, you might write a long checklist of all the things that need to be done to achieve a particular outcome–an outcome that, of course, your new offer makes simpler, faster, and easier. The point of the email is to show just how hard it is to 'do without' your product.

Notice how from just these first two examples, you'll be writing completely different emails?

Totally different vibes, right?

These different hooks tell you what to write about *and* make sure that each email feels fresh, resetting your readers' attention.

Why Planning Hooks is Crucial

By planning the hooks first, you can guide your readers

along a logical and emotional journey towards buying what you're selling.

- You won't leave out any important points.
- You won't repeat yourself.
- You'll have a clear direction for your entire campaign.

This kind of clarity, your subscribers can;t get confused. And that means they'll buy.

This is all done by planning *what* you're going to be saying, not *how* you're going to say it.

It's done by planning the theme of each email, not by stressing over specific words you'll use to say something.

Think of it like a teacher preparing lessons. They don't script the exact words they'll say in class, but they plan the lessons that move students through the curriculum, so they build an understanding of the subject day after day.

All you have to do is make sure the words you DO write stay on course .Each email only delivers on that one hook.

Planning Your Email Campaign

Now, when you create a new campaign, plan it out before writing a single word.

Whip open a new Google Doc and decide:

1. How many days your campaign will run
2. The number of emails you'll send each day
3. The hook for each email

These three elements move your readers through a structured journey where they:

- Understand your offer
- Get more excited about it
- Feel compelled to buy it.

No magic, clever words alone will ever do that. Instead, these completely invisible, uncopyable things are the three big levers that do most of the work.

It amazes me how many people waste time trying to be better copywriters, trying to use better, more persuasive words to make sales, instead of structuring effective campaigns.

The hook is what makes the biggest difference.

Those folks are trying to breed faster horses, when in fact what they need is an automobile.

So forget about whether you're good with words. Focus on what your audience needs to understand to move from their current mindset to buying your solution.

Just write sincerely.

Plan the journey they need to go through. Then simply use the best words you have and you'll already be flying past the wordsmiths on their thoroughbred ponies...in your sportscar.

But which offers should you make in your emails, and in what order?

ACTION:
Create strategic email campaigns by designing the hooks first and then writing the emails.

The 'Mother Framework' gives you the core framework of every email campaign, the essential beats to hit and how to manage the 'middle dip' of any campaign sequence. You can download it using the QR code:

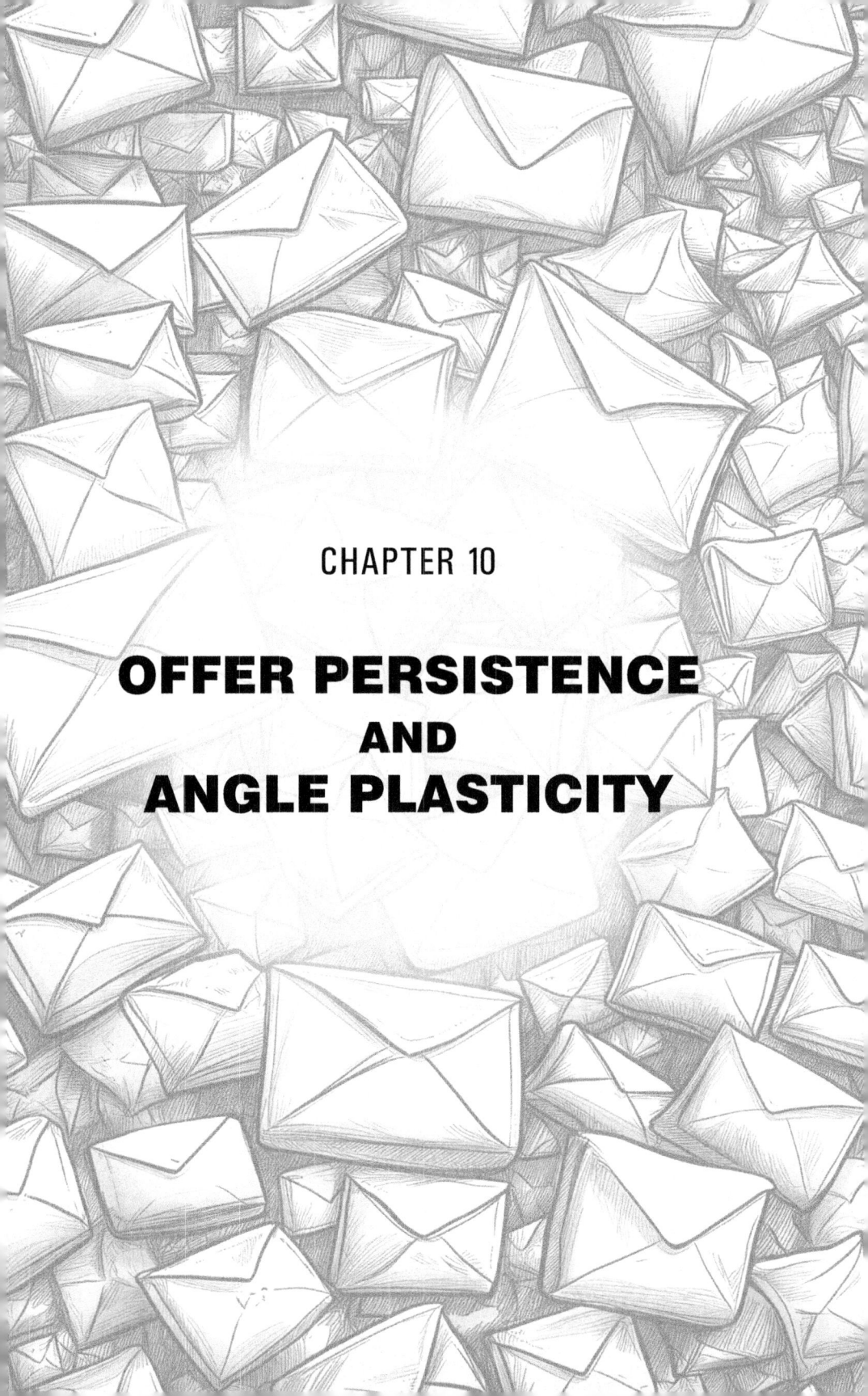

CHAPTER 10

OFFER PERSISTENCE AND ANGLE PLASTICITY

He's got a little monkey on his outstretched hand and he's shouting "Monkey?"

I look confused.

"Some pencils? How about a rug? An elephant statue?"

That was my first-and only-trip to Egypt.

I was working as a fly-on Entertainer on a Holland America Line cruise ship and we'd docked in the port of Alexandria. On my way from the ship to the bus, we passed through the wooden terminal, and the guy running the shop was putting all his energy into offering me a whole range of things I might want.

His effort was admirable. He didn't want me to leave without buying *something*. Anything, really.

Yes, he did open with 'monkey'. But maybe that was just to get my attention. Maybe.

Perhaps I should have asked about the price of the monkey. I don't know.

But here's the question for you: what *did* I buy from our Egyptian trader?

Any guesses?

Answer: Nothing. Not a thing.

And it's not because he didn't have anything I wanted–I don't think.

See, if he'd spent the time to tell me more about how the monkey is friendly, showed me how it makes a cracking cup of tea, got me to imagine the viral social content I'd create with him and then explained how to easily transport it back to the UK, he might have had a much better chance.

Opening up with the monkey, an outrageous offer like this combines a few powerful psychological principles we can learn from. So, before I talk shit about this chap, let's appreciate what he nailed:

1. **Attention.** His opening offer was wild enough for me to stop at his little stall. Your opening gambit needs to do the same - grab attention.

2. **Framing.** Starting with something as outrageous as a monkey made his follow-up offers (pencils, rugs) seem much more reasonable. This technique works well in marketing. Start by initially offering a high-price, high-commitment offer that a small percentage of people will take. But it's not there to be bought. It's there to make the next offers seem like an easier yes.

That's regular marketing stuff. So, let's get into the advanced stuff.

The Advanced Lesson: Persistence and Familiarity

Fellow marketer and webinar royalty, Jason Fladlien shared that the first time someone hears an offer, they're going to say no. (Listen to our conversation when he joined me on *The Email Marketing Show Podcast* on Spotify and everywhere else you get podcasts these days).

Jason's point of getting that first 'no' out the way is spot on–it shows the value of persistence.

Look at TV ads. Brands like Coca-Cola and McDonald's keep running their ads for years–and they keep changing the ads. But it's still the same product, just with different offers. Why?

It uses the equation:

$$\text{TIME} \times \text{RESONANCE}$$

Time builds familiarity. Humans like things that feel familiar, which is why big brands keep reinforcing the same product. The more familiar it feels, the more we start believing that *we* are choosing to buy.

Resonance is when the message clicks with us.

The great news is that if you're going to spend more time talking about the same offer, you'll also need to find new angles to talk about it from, so it resonates with different people.

And better still, offer persistence is the fastest and cheapest way to more money.

Oh hello—got your attention, have I?

Look, when you *move on* from one offer to the next one, you have to create a new offer. Each new offer means building the product or service, creating new marketing assets, and figuring out the messaging and sales process from scratch. This can be slow-going... and expensive.

But coming up with new angles for the same offer? That's faster, cheaper, and far more effective. The next chapter will dig into how to do this easily.

ACTION:

Keep promoting your one offer longer, but from more angles. Instead of switching products, come up with fresh new angles and offers for that one product. This way, you maximise understanding and sales—while reducing the need to create more products.

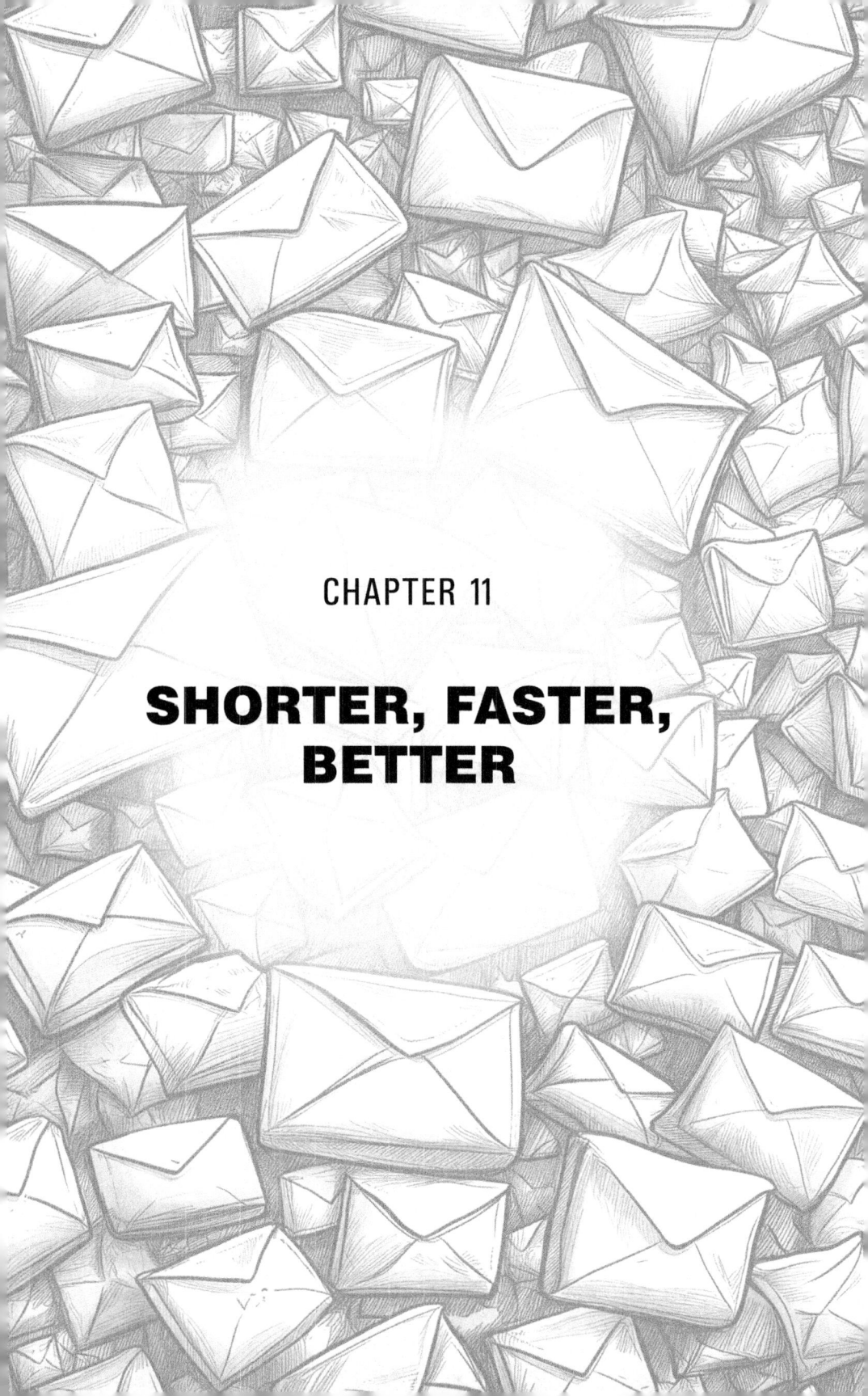

CHAPTER 11

SHORTER, FASTER, BETTER

I've got something that will increase how many people click the links in your emails, how many people read your emails, give you more ideas for more emails you can send *and* make them faster to write–all at once.

That seems like a lot for one short chapter to deliver on, but all of these things can happen when you implement what I've got for you here.

Focusing Your Emails

We know that different people buy for different reasons, right? Some people need to see the testimonials first and others won't buy until they've got some kind of risk reversal. Some want to see someone just like them having success before they commit.

And, of course, what we need to see changes for each product we buy, the price point, and our previous purchasing experiences.

That's why emails and sales pages include promises, evidence, social proof, risk reversals and all that stuff, right?

We know that.

Okay, so now to make my point, let me share a fact that annoys the shit out of me...

In the USA, there's a picture puzzle game called *Where's Waldo?*

But in the UK, the same thing is called *Where's Wally?*

Someone in the marketing department either didn't think Americans could cope with the name 'Wally', or that us Brits couldn't possibly believe the name 'Waldo'.

Either way, we're all expected to believe in his daft costume that he wears on every occasion. It doesn't matter whether this dumb guy who can't use Maps is lost at the beach or in a city, a park, or in a mine - he's wearing that stupid suit. And spectacles.

Anyway, that's my rant about this little prick out of the way.[4]

Here's what we do know - the game of Where's Dumbass Wally-Waldo is about finding this guy in a sea of other people and things that look a lot like him.

---

4   I hate him. I really hate him. His smug little face. The way he convinces tons of people to dress up in clothes just like him just so he can play his silly game. I hope he wears those glasses when he opens the oven door and they get all steamed up. Shithead.

Finding him in those chaotic scenes takes ages.

And, in an all too similar manner, the big mistake I see with emails is people putting too much in a single email, burying their point. That means they're playing Wheres-What's-His-Name with every one of the points they're trying to make.

And poor readers/subscribers on the other end of that email can't see the transformational outcome, because it's hidden in a sea of benefits, testimonials, and urgency–who are all wearing that same red and white striped hat as Wally/Waldo.

The Big Mistake: Overstuffing Your Emails (And What to do Instead)

I see emails all the time that introduce the offer, describe the discount, and explain the payment plan- all in *one* email. That's *at least* three emails in one.

We can create more, interesting and compelling emails if we take each of those things and break them out into separate messages:

- ⊙ One email announces the offer.
- ⊙ Another highlights the discount.
- ⊙ A third covers the payment plan.

Think about the difference between that 700-word email and three-much shorter-separate emails. Overwhelm is real and overloading someone's mind with lots of different points means none of them properly sinks in.

This works because it ends with:

- **Clearer focus**: One point per email keeps your message clear and memorable.

- **Shorter emails:** One point per email means those emails are quicker to read and super consumable. With attention spans being stretched thinner and thinner, snappier emails are also much more likely to be read. (I know when I get a long email I have to mark it to come back and read later. Which I mostly forget to do. So it never gets read.)

- **Increased engagement:** Shorter emails also means that if you have a call to action-say, a link that you want people to click in the email-people are much more likely to make it to that call to action. With longer emails... Well, let me put it this way: How can someone really click a link if they don't make it to the bottom of the email?

It's amazing, some emails feel like one of those wells you find in the middle of nowhere– you toss a coin in and never hear it hit the bottom.

Yeah, that coin is your readers' attention.

It's falling into darkness and it might not make it.

Shorter Emails = Faster Writing (and More Consistent Emails)

One of my favorite things about shorter emails above everything is that they're faster to write.

So many people put off doing more email stuff because their emails are long. And if my emails were long, I'd put off doing them, too.

On average, our emails are 175 words. Total.

How?

Because each email makes one point. That's it.

Not only does this keep the writing brief, but it also streamlines the thinking process. It's not like writing this book where I'm weaving ideas together in ways to keep your attention and make them link beautifully.

If you know this email has to only tell people that you just put up a new video they should check out...guess what? That's all you're going to say in that email.

In the email about how 'Sheila took her email list of 74 people and makes over $100,000 with our Temptress Campaign' - that is the ONLY thing that email will talk about.

Your mind can't get distracted by having to change thoughts and link things together. You have one job, and one job only–driving your *one* point home to the reader, in the most efficient way possible.

Those two things make writing emails faster.

And hooray for writing them faster.

As a dyslexic, I find that particularly satisfying.

Here's the thing–we're all busy, right?

You are. I am. Your readers are.

And that means we're all seeing lots of messages, lots of emails, lots of social posts.

By breaking your points into multiple emails, you create more opportunities for your audience to engage. Instead of sending one overloaded email that might get overlooked, you can send several focused emails - over six days.

We asked a stats guy to go into our email system and do some analysis stuff, and what he discovered blew me away.

If I was going to write this as a headline, it would read something like:

How We Get an 85% Email Open Rate Every Single Week

Yep, you read that right. **Our open rate on individual emails is about 30% (fairly average) but because we email daily, 85% of our subscribers open an email every week.**

If we didn't have much to say, by blowing it all in one, two, or three emails for example, we would not be having that kind of impact on our people.

Now, let's get practical.

You start off by writing down the *hook* of the email you're going to write (flip back to chapter 9 if you need a refresher on this).

Having that hook at the top of the page focuses you and keeps you on track with only writing about that one point..

For example, one of the hooks in our *Overture Sales Sequence* is 'The Popular Contradiction.'

That means in this email, the only thing you're allowed to talk about is some piece of common wisdom that you can prove is not true. That you stand against.

For example, we might write one about the fact that most people think subject lines are what get your emails opened. They're not. And we'll go on to explain why that's the case. (You're curious now, aren't you? Worry thee not, we're coming onto that in a couple of chapters' time.)

This is all made much easier to do if you write the hooks out first, like we discussed back in Chapter 9, and the *only* thing you do is speak to that hook.

Doing this keeps your emails focused, you can't draw a blank, keeps them snappy and short *and* it makes sure your email campaign flows together to move people towards buying, rather than being random emails in a random order.

Our template for writing emails in the right order makes this really simple and even makes writing the subject line so much easier. I've popped the template for you at EmailMarketingBook.com/email-plan

ACTION:

Take one of the recent emails you've sent out and analyze it–be critical. How long is it? Stick it into a Google doc and review the word count. Then, break it up into multiple shorter emails. Make just *one point* in each email and keep those emails *super short*–150 - 300 words. This way, people will read them and the point will stand out much stronger.

17 Point Email Content Score Card. These are the 17 points that I judge every email by, to know whether it'll be successful. (It's also how I judge whether what A.I. produces is any good). Check your emails against my 17-point score card, just scan the QR code with your phone:

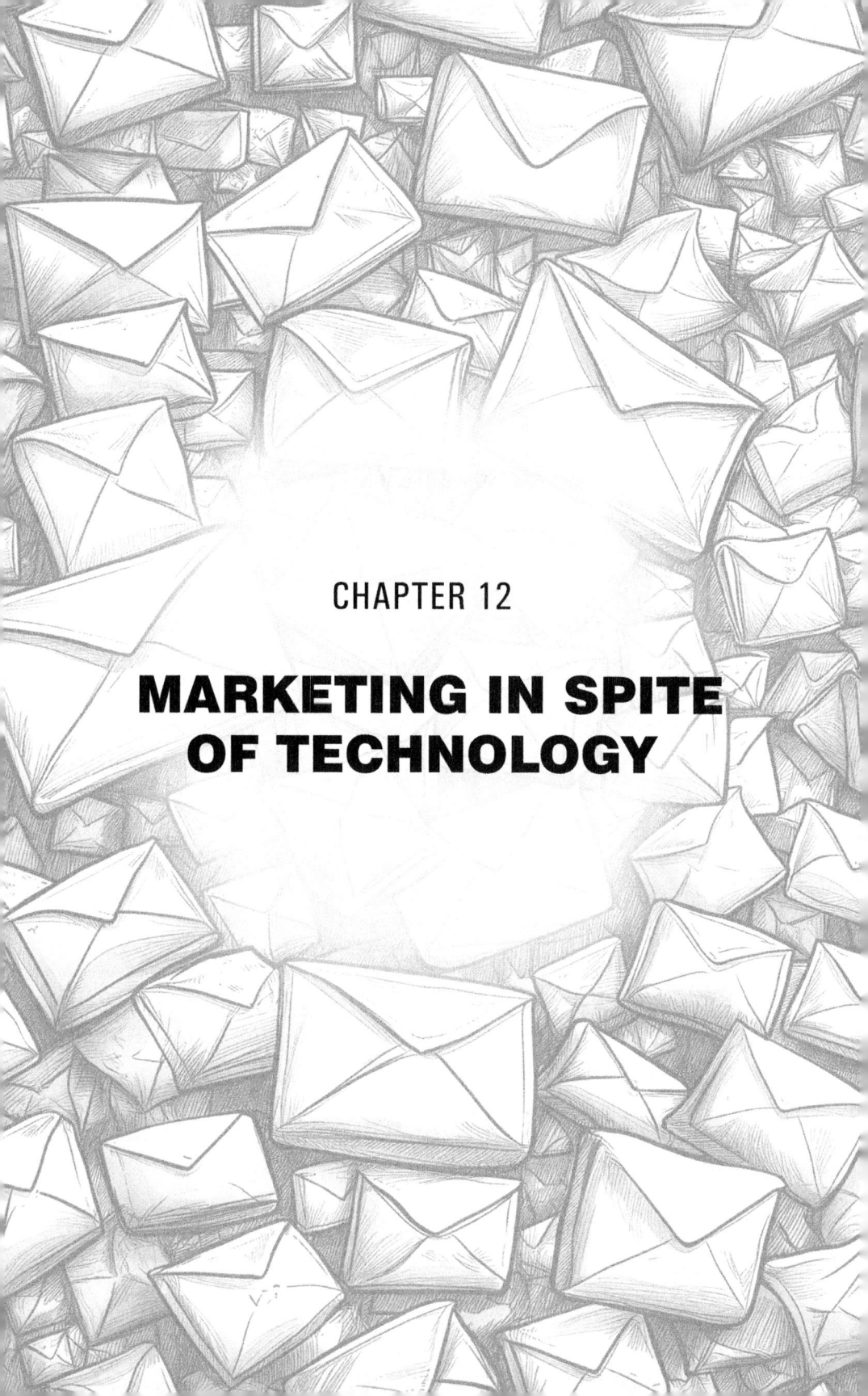

CHAPTER 12

MARKETING IN SPITE OF TECHNOLOGY

How blue is the sky?

If I asked you that question how might you answer it?

Good news is, there's a thing called a Cyanometer.

This isn't a new piece of tech. It is a 230-year-old tool that is designed to answer that question. Cool, ey?

How does it work? Absolutely no idea.

How it works isn't important.

Just use it and get the result.

My dad used to have this toolbox full of stuff he almost never used.

And that's the key–*almost*.

Because whenever something needed doing around the house, he'd fetch his dusty, rusting old tool box that he'd had all his life and he'd have 'just the tool for the job'.

I bloody miss my dad every day. And I have no idea what ever happened to that rusty old box full of 'the tools for every job'.

A lot of people start off by thinking that email marketing is about tools. They think it's about technology.

When in truth, the tech is just the thing that *assists* you in doing the things you plan on doing. The things you want to do to get the job done best.

That's really important for us to remember, especially when we've had one of those days when the bastard thing isn't playing nice or messes up.

But really, a builder doesn't order a hammer, nails and some bricks and then start wondering what to build.

We start off with the plan. We architect an email campaign, we design an email strategy so that our campaigns all work together. And only then do we get the tool to make our plan happen.

Our process for planning email campaigns and strategies uses the simplest of all tools:

1. A piece of paper - or more recently an iPad because it's easier to adjust and share.
2. A Google Doc - because we can collaborate and share content super easily.

The first step is to draw out the journey from a subscriber's point of view on the paper/iPad.

Draw it out.

What do THEY see?

Please, not 'what you *do to them*'.

What is *their* experience?

They opt in to your list and then what...?

The first thing we map out is what they do.

Then we go back and ask at each junction, "What if they don't (do the thing I expect them to do)?"

HINT: These 'what if they don't' areas are massive opportunities for profit.

Everyone seems to fall in love with 'they'll do this and then that, and then that...' but the truth is...most people won't.

They won't click that link.

They won't watch the video.

They won't register.

They won't buy.

They won't attend.

They won't upgrade.

They won't book in.

I'm just going to tell you the truth. Statistically speaking, most people will not do what you want them to do.

That's why asking 'what if they don't' at each step of the way is where you can pick up, close gaps and help more people to buy from you.

With this mapped out, we then go into a Google Doc and one person comes up with the hooks for each email - we talked about that in an earlier chapter - and then they write the emails.

Next, they send it around the team members involved for their suggestions.

When working on solo projects, each of those 'people' is me. I write the first draft then take a short break to make a cup of tea, go for a short walk, or just rub one of that cat's bellies.

Now, in 'Suggestions Mode' in Google Docs, we make changes, suggestions and sometimes write hilarious commentary.

Finally, the owner of the document can accept changes, dispute them and tidy out any loose bits.

Hopefully at this point it's clear that we've drawn out the campaign and we've written the emails as we'd like it to all work.

Notice how NONE of this actually involved even logging in to your email marketing platform.

Since I know only a small percentage of people will have read this much of the book, it's only the people who this email marketing stuff is really important to who get it - so I'm going to share something with you.

There is an old saying that if you want to keep a secret, write it in a book. So, here goes...

I create a ton of email strategies, I've developed and created a LOT of email campaigns, and I've written thousands of emails.

But until about 3 months ago, I did not have the login for our email marketing platform.

Why?

I didn't need one.

(Recently I started some project work and wanted to go deep into some tech stuff so finally got myself an account.)

You see, email marketing is about the strategy and the hooks. It's about the beliefs you're building and the journey you're taking people on.

If you allow yourself to write and plan your email marketing in your email platform, you're automatically throttling your creativity by the platform capabilities vs what you want. Meaning, you're restricting yourself to what you think can be done with the tech tool in front of you.

When you're planning and writing your email marketing you must do it outside of your platform. This way, you can do whatever you want. You can do what's best for your subscriber and what will get the best results for your sales.

That's what I do.

I decide what I want to happen without any consideration for how to do it.

I'm a dreamer. I dream up impossible magic tricks with an utter disregard for how they could be possible.

That way, I can dream bigger. I can dream *better*.

Then, once the campaign is planned and written, suggestions are accepted and signed off on--the team goes about building it.

Take, for instance, when we were away in Portugal for a business getaway last summer. We're sitting outside of the villa, around the pool planning the marketing for our Email Hero Blueprint and I came up with an idea for a campaign where we give people the first module of the program for free.

That way they can log in, watch it, enjoy it *and* they get to experience what it's like to be a customer of the product.

Everyone loved the idea and we poured some more drinks!

A month or so later, I wrote the emails into a Google Doc and then it wasn't until a few months after that we had a meeting to figure out how to actually do it.

The idea and the writing of the emails were all happening without any consideration for technology, for whether things were even possible.

It was all created from the perspective of what I wanted to do. What my vision was, as it were.

Of course, I know how email platforms work so I will often stick my two cents in about how I think it could be done.

But here's the thing.

The email platform should never steer or inspire your email marketing.

Your spade doesn't help you design the house.

You design your email marketing and then you bend the tool to your will.

If it means creating workarounds, do it.

If it means a piece of extra software, get it.

You designed an email campaign that you think will work.

You thought it through carefully.

So the thinking is sound and complete.

Of course there are limitations with all tools. Every platform has stuff it cannot do. When you hit that will, there are two really important ways to deal with it:

1. Find a workaround and compromise a tiny little bit. Maybe get add-on tools.

2. If the flaw is something you know other platforms can do, but yours can't seem to do it - change platform.

I realise that second point is pretty direct and flippant, but I mean it.

Over the past 5 years in particular there has been an alarming number of new email platforms launched into the market.

Most of them have a feature set that's nice enough if you're a small, part-time hobby business.

But notice that none of the professional businesses out there who are making multiple 6-figures, 7-figures and more are using those platforms.

You've got this far through reading this book about email marketing. That's a lot of effort you've put in, so you know this stuff is important.

And here's what blows my tiny little fucking mind every day:

People join programs, they read books and they study email marketing because they say that they realise they have to make more from their email marketing. They know it's the lifeblood of the whole entire sales part of their business.

Yet they are still using a tool that is *stopping* them from doing what needs to be done or at very least making it harder than it needs to be.

That's important, so let me say that again in a bolder font:

They Are Still Using a Tool That is *Stopping* Them From Doing What Needs to be Done.

I'm right handed, I'm never going to buy a left handed pair of scissors or else I'd just never wrap a gift again.

If you want to get fit and lose some weight, you don't lock your fitness clothes in the attic. You place them within easy reach to reduce the resistance to doing what needs to be done.

Then why would anyone continue using a tool that makes this stuff harder?

Get the tool that makes doing this stuff easiest.

There are like 5 of them on the market and you know which they are.

They're the ones who:

1. *Use tags.* If it doesn't use tags, it's not up to standard. End of.

2. *Have a visual automation builder.* Automations are annoying enough to figure out the logic of, so any system that has no automation in it or uses 'if this then that' statement blocks to do the logic of their automation - get out. In an email system today, that's more work.

3. *Integrate with other tools.* We live in a world where we want things to connect and talk to each other so you can be in control of systemising automatic and simplifying things. If your email system doesn't have what's called an API to connect to other things, it's holding you back.

Those 3 things are critical. If your current email marketing platform doesn't have them, you need to switch systems to have genuine success with email marketing.

Why?

Because the platform needs to serve you.

If you cannot segment people, create automations and connect it to other tools you're using, then it's not going to serve you as well as the great tools that do.

And I know we now have two camps of people at this point.

We have those who use a system that does all of these things (and much more) who are thinking 'well, obviously' and we have the people who have put up a wall or are worried about switching platforms.

Good news, if you're in that second group - the sooner you move, the easier it is and because your current solution wasn't doing all of those things, it's less work to move than if all those things were set up.

After that tough love, I want to bring it down a bit and pull out a comfy bean bag for you to sit on as I share this with you:

There are two problems with tech that has these limitations:

- The first is that the limitations themselves are making you physically unable to do all of the things you plan and want to do. All because 'my platform cannot do that'.

- The second, is that these limitations squash your creativity - so your *thinking* becomes limited.

The platform should serve your plans, your subscribers and your sales. If it can't, then it's time to switch to a platform that can.

Which platforms do I mean?

Well, since these platforms are changing all the time and we don't want to give you outdated information - you deserve the truth - so we keep a live rundown of the platforms and what we recommend online. And as a reader of this book you can go check it out by scanning the QR code at the end of this chapter.

ACTION:

Plan your marketing campaigns on paper and write them in documents so you can plan the best marketing possible. Evaluate your current email marketing platform and if it doesn't serve you, get one that will. And then see how to make your technology do what you've designed.

Email Platforms Showdown is where I show you what is hot, and what is NOT, in various email platforms. This is a living, breathing resource I keep up to date with what the platforms are releasing, updating and of course new platforms that enter the space. Get access to this live resource and see which email platforms stack up by scanning the QR code with your phone:

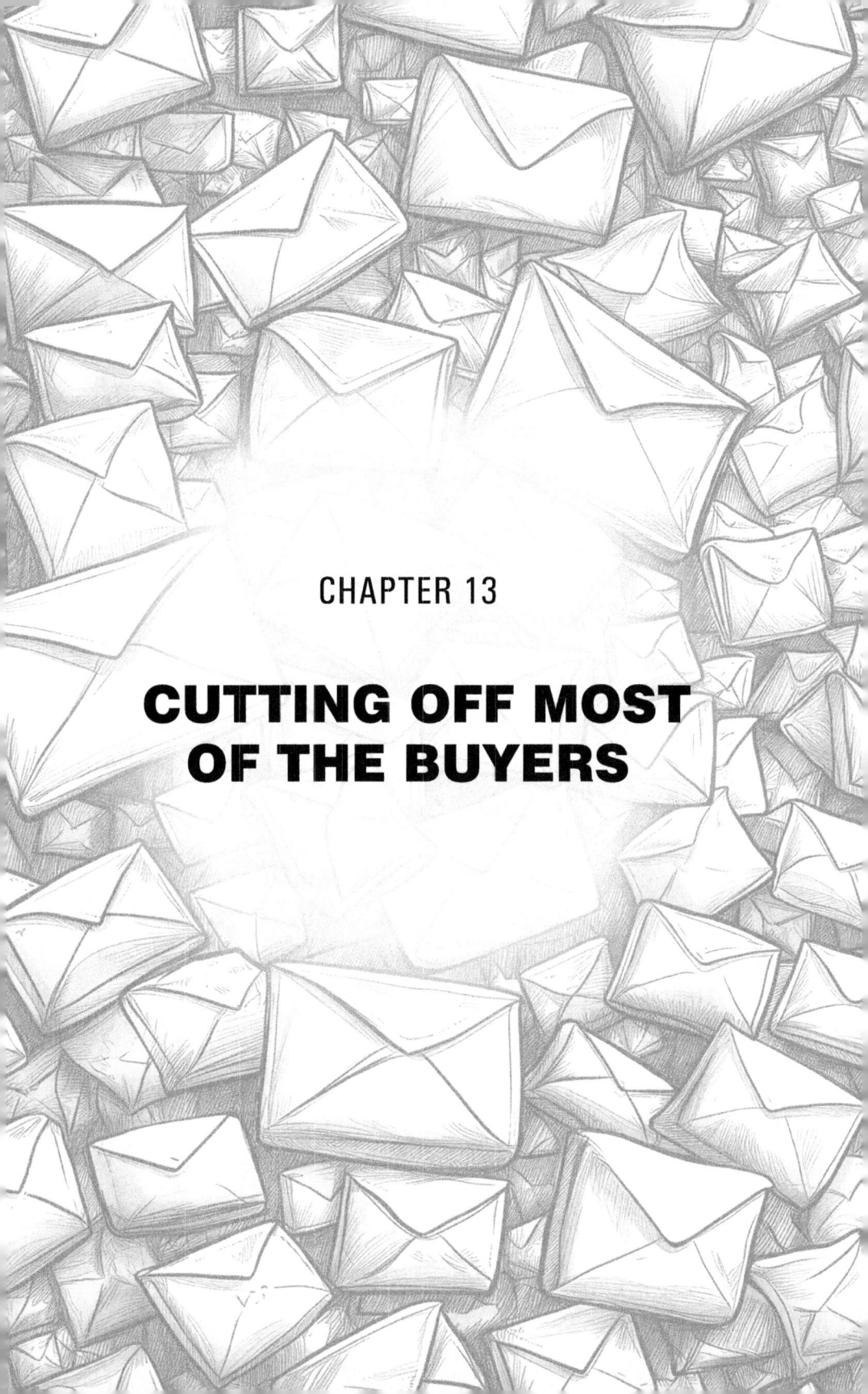

CHAPTER 13

CUTTING OFF MOST OF THE BUYERS

Have you ever run a sale or offered a discount to your list and had 100% of people buy?

(Me neither, by the way. This isn't one of those 'well I can show you how if you hold my magic stick' stories.)

Yet, when most people want to boost sales, they default to offering a discount to their list. As if the price is the only thing stopping them from buying.

I've run discounts and made *no* sales before.

Why?

Because I didn't understand an important thing about human behaviours.

That's behaviours–with an 's'.

Different People, Different Motivations

I once bought a new robot vacuum cleaner because there was $300 off it in some Amazon deal. I was actually perfectly happy with the one we had. But that deal did make me spend money when I wasn't planning on it.

I'm human like everyone else who's buying stuff, right?

But I don't always buy things based on them being discounted.

CUTTING OFF MOST OF THE BUYERS

I bought a course about DJing because it came with a free second course. It wasn't the *free* portion that grabbed my attention there, but rather the fact I could get twice the knowledge for something I was invested in at the time.

I hired a friend of mine for a day's consulting and flew to her house in Austin, Texas because she is the one person I trusted to help me take my business to the next stage.

When buying tickets to see Imagine Dragons there's no discount, but I rushed to buy them before they sold out.

I've pre-ordered that new video game for my PS5 because I want to play it on the day it's released.

My point is, we buy different things for different reasons.

Yet when we look at the email campaigns that many of the internet marketing gurus share and sell, they are almost all discounts.

"Get this bundle of things for less than one of them costs."

"Get my $997 course for just $27"

"Special flash sale."

"I'm doing an experiment, so it's a crazy price, get it now before I come to my senses."

And other mozzarella-drenched baloney.

Yes, we all want to get a good deal.

And we all want to get more value than how much we spend on the thing.

Sure, discounts work. We all love a good deal. But the real reason so many marketers rely on discounts is *they don't know what else to do.*

The key is understanding that people buy for different reasons.

So instead of showing up to your superfans and offering a discount, you can keep that extra money and appeal to their desire for what's new, fresh, and interesting.

For everyone else, certainty is key. That's where you actually have to do some marketing and that's where appealing just to that one buying motivator (such a discounting) becomes stale and eventually invisible.

"Does he ever sell anything at the price it's supposed to be?"

That's what's in the back of people's subconscious minds, gnawing away at their trust levels. Eventually causing them to stop even reading the emails.

(Remember; we're always training our subscribers' behaviours.)

Building Trust Through Risk Reversal

Instead of a discount (again), offer a radical risk reversal to capture their attention..

You'll especially have the attention of the people who have bought things from other people in the past and been burned and disappointed by those purchases.

Imagine Eric.

Eric has seen the fancy sales page before, it's got a lovely layout, popping video and all the big promises of how this is going to solve his problems.

He took a leap of faith. He even asked his partner if it's okay to spend money on this thing. He dug through 5 pairs of jeans to see which pocket he left his wallet in and fumbled through entering the credit card details.

He found his phone and verified the payment.

His excitement fueled him through all of those steps.

At each point, Eric could have given up.

But the guy on the page said he could help them. *"The guy on the page is going to make all my problems go away."*

So Eric pushed himself over each of those hurdles, justified it to his partner, and invested.

Only to find that when he logged in, it was some shitty 24-minute video with crappy sound that tells them they need to buy the next thing.

He's deflated.

Eric is embarrassed that he fell for it.

And now, playing that back in his mind he's here, staring at YOUR page. And he's scared of feeling stupid again. So, he's hesitating.

But Embarrassed Eric is not alone. He lives in a terraced house, next door to Frustrated Fred.

(I don't know why their parents gave them such awfully inhibiting names. But that's Dickhead Dorothy and Pricky Pete for you.)

Fred is also hesitating. His mouse cursor is hovering over the 'buy' button.

Fred believes you. He's seen the testimonials. He's seen the case studies. He sees how you help people go from point A, to point B.

But Fred isn't as good as you. He isn't as smart or experienced as all those other people.

And he looks through his inbox at all those courses he's bought before. He's tried really hard to make them work. But he's just not good at it.

He's just not *good enough* to make it work for him.

He knows it's not your fault.

It's him.

Thing is, you have Erics and Freds in your email list. And while a discount might get them to think about taking a risk, what they really need is another reason to buy that overcomes their situation. They need **certainty**—a reason to trust that this time, things will be different.

This is not a lesson to say 'don't discount'. It is about reminding us all that discounting is just one tool. It appeals to one buying type.

Other people will buy because something is exclusive. It is limited in access.

I'm known for spending what some would say are 'outrageous amounts' on designer aftershaves.

Turns out I buy aftershave on exclusivity.

There's loads of people who sell knockoff 'smells just like' aftershaves. I won't buy them.

Because I'm not buying for the discount when I'm shopping for aftershave.

I'm buying because I know that I have a real legitimate bottle of Creed. And it's special.

Some people are like that with watches, others with cars.

One of our mentors has a special very limited edition swipe file of marketing campaigns he's been collecting for over a decade. It's *special*.

Those things aren't going to go on sale and be offered at a discount, are they?

This is why in our email sequences we cycle through 5 different buying triggers to make the same offer.

And the beautiful thing here is that appealing to more buying triggers gives you even more opportunities for more emails about your core Rome Offer.

See how all of this is coming together?

(And while this might feel like a stream of consciousness from a guy high on meds, I can assure you–I've not taken my meds.)

> **ACTION:**
> **Build email campaigns that appeal to different buying triggers. Not everyone buys for the same reason, and understanding those differences is the key to stronger sales and happier customers.**

The Buyer Triggers. There are 5 major Buyer Triggers that cause different people to buy different things. When you use all 5 of them you stack up sales (we multiplied ours by 18x, for example). I've put together a training on those Buyer Triggers for you, just scan the QR code with your phone:

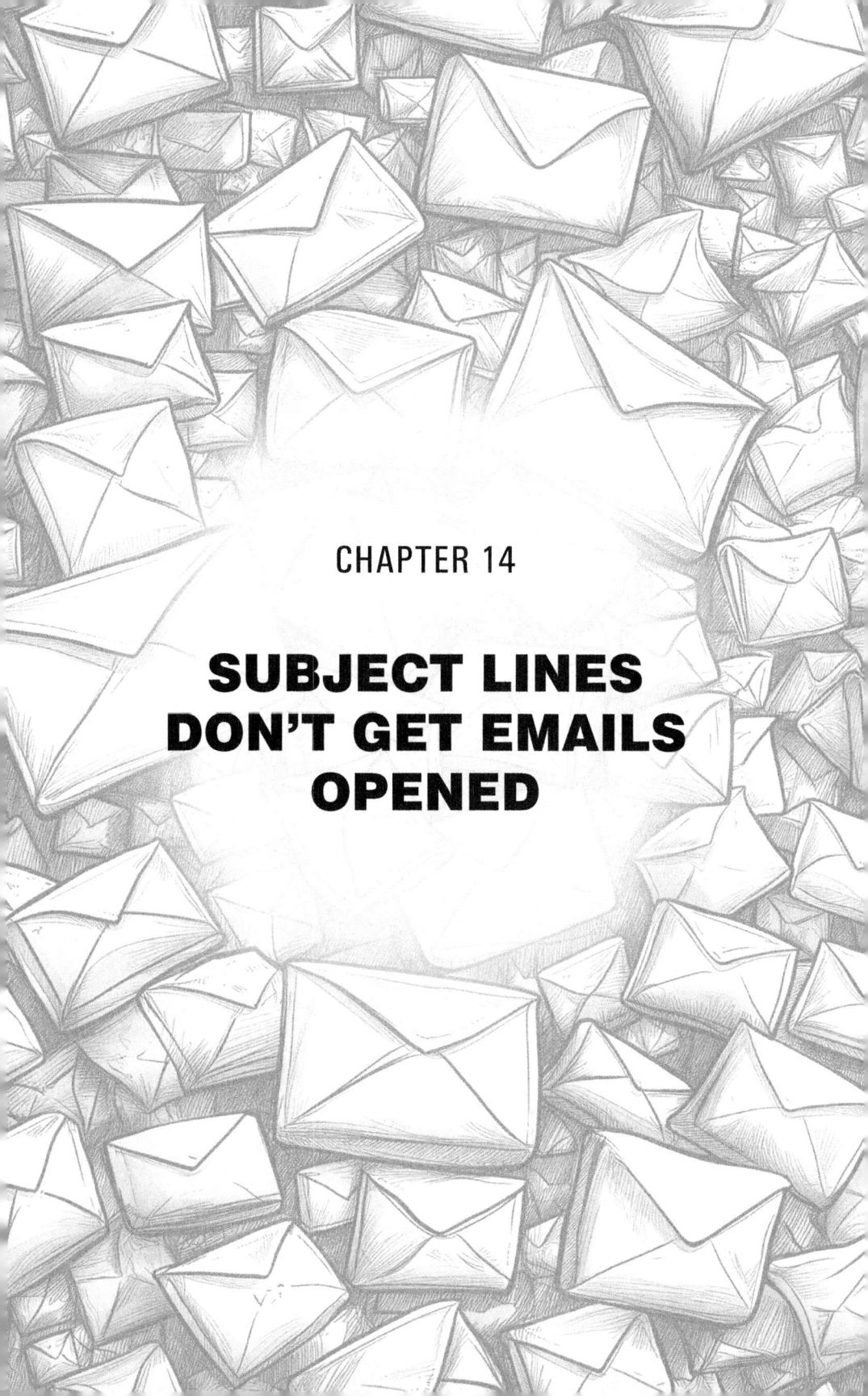

CHAPTER 14

SUBJECT LINES DON'T GET EMAILS OPENED

How do you increase your email open rate?

The standard answer to this question is to "test the subject lines." Try different ones. Try more provocative ones.

And while subject line testing *can* improve how many emails get opened, it's not the big lever.

Throughout this time we've been spending together, we've been looking for the BIG levers in email marketing. (The automobiles, not the faster horses.)

And open rates are one of those perpetually misunderstood things that almost no one seems to have properly questioned.

Being the contrarians we are, we did.

Before we get into what really increases open rates, let's not poopoo subject lines entirely. Because they DO serve a very important purpose.

And we have a method for writing unlimited subject lines that are unique and non-formulaic. So they stand out and do their job. (More on that in a moment.)

The Real Job of a Subject Line

A subject line's job isn't to get the email opened–it's to set people up for the click.

Okay, I know this contradicts pretty much everything you've been told about subject lines. Stay with me.

We analysed thousands of emails and saw significant amounts of them getting lower open rates but higher click-throughs. (In plain English, less people are opening, but more of those people are clicking to check out the offer.)

And that's what we want.

Email marketing is like a relay race:

- The job of the email is to get people to click the link.
- The job of the sales page is to get them to the cart.
- The job of the cart is to take the money.

Each piece has its own singular purpose. We call this 'Passing the Baton'.

This thinking really helps simplify what we're trying to do with our email, doesn't it?

But it's been a longstanding mistake to think that the job of the subject line is to get the email opened. And to get *that* achieved, people will do anything– including tricking their subscribers with misleading subject lines.

A subject line that tricks someone into opening the email has achieved the job of getting the email opened. But that's not its job.

That's like your dentist coming over to fix the tiles on the roof. Not his job.

They both have tools and drills and things, but you don't want a roofer rummaging around in your mouth.

You can use any old thing to trick people to open emails. And you see it all the time.

From people who should know better.

But those people are playing the numbers game. They're playing a game of having a huge email list and making faster horses.

That's not the game we're playing.

We're playing the 'maximum conversion from however big your email list is' game.

Imagine receiving an email with the subject line:

Sale #18689 - $197

If you didn't just buy something for $197, then you're going to open it out of curiosity.

Then you read:

"Imagine having $197 sales dropping into your account every hour, even when you're sleeping..."

And it goes on to tell you about the latest trick or hack to 'make money while you sleep with no skill, no list, only needing a taco and a toenail'...

How do you feel?

Tricked.

Deceived.

Disappointed.

And you curse yourself for falling for it.

Your level of trust for the nitwit who sent you that email completely tanked.

And you know next time you get *any* email from that person, you're going to expect to be let down and be way less excited to open it.

The emotion you associate with that person will forever be disappointment. And if this person is letting you down just with the emails they send, how are they with their paid products?

But if you get someone to open an email and deliver on what you said, then you build trust. Credibility. And credibility means more opens over time.

I'll give you that big lever for increasing open rates in a moment, but first, we do need to talk subject lines.

The Right Way to Use Subject Lines

You see, emails have to have subject lines so we should put something really good in there.

(Although fun fact: one of my highest open-rate subject lines ever was 'no subject'.)

We want to stand out. We want to have people thinking, 'Damn, I have to open and read that.'

The old approach was to use benefit-driven subject lines. You know, to appeal to the natural self interest of human beings. To show them what's in it for them, how it's going to help them.

E.g.: "How we made $10k yesterday", "When to start your New Year's resolutions", "Is THIS how to invest now?"

Quick History Lesson...

This technique came from direct response 'junk mail' marketing. Marketers used to add what's called 'teaser copy' to the outside of the envelopes to entice people to open them..When email came around, they lifted that 'teaser copy' idea and made it the subject line.

But this approach has three major problems

1. We're all much more aware of marketing tactics today, so when these subject lines have a heavy stench of marketing instead of curiosity and excitement of the Teaser Copy Era, our resistance goes up.

2. Every one of the *other* 120 people we get emails from each day (on average) is using the same formula, so they just blend in. Instead of standing out.

3. They're not the best way of getting the most engagement from people.

What to Use Instead: The Compound Curiosity Method

The technique we created for writing non-formulaic subject lines is called Compound Curiosity.

This thing is so simple, but it means literally anyone can write subject lines that people want to know more about. (We do have a full training on exactly how to create these, but you can use the fundamentals right now.)

The idea? Include at least TWO elements of curiosity in your subject line.

At *least* two.

Let me show you the difference between a standard, lukewarm curiosity subject line and a white-hot Compound Curiosity subject line:

Curiosity:

Subj: My girlfriend is going to flip

The only curious thing here is "what is their girlfriend going to flip about?"

Compound Curiosity:

Subj: She's going to flip.

There's a lot of curiosity in this one, right?

- Who's going to flip?
- What are they going to flip about?
- Is it a good type of 'flip' or a bad type of 'flip'?
- What will I think?

By switching this one word('girlfriend' to 'she'), the subject line changed from a regular curiosity subject line into a compelling, curiosity-layered one that people want to open. It has too many unknowns that our brain cannot accept or even come up with some possible outcomes for.

So yes, subject lines do help with getting people to open our emails.

You see, generally we want to steer away from giving away the whole story in the subject line. Which people do all too often, leaving no reason to open the email. (Which is easily avoided with Compound Curiosity subject lines.)

But sometimes, we want to tell the whole story in the subject line because we want people to know something even if they don't open the email.

Think about that: even if *they don't open* the email.

What are people seeing from you if they just scroll down their inbox? What's the narrative?

So generally, you'll want to spell things out clearly in situations like:

- 'Offer closes in 60-mins'
- 'My New Book Launches Now'
- 'Live class link (inside)'

In all of these situations, the direct subject lines are great to make sure the message is heard loud and clear.

Balancing direct subject lines and Compound Curiosity subject lines helps appeal to different people with different psychological motivators.

The Biggest Lever For Open Rates

Now that you've got a handle on how we do subject lines–let's look at the big lever you can pull to increase your open rates dramatically.

It's one that a lot of people won't like. But it's not a trick. Nor a hack.

It's *trust*.

Think about it: I've only ever had one email from my mother, or Mam as we call her here in the North East of England. It was to send me some documents I needed when I bought my first house.

But Mam is not much of an emailer so she forgot to put the subject line in before she sent it to me.

The email landed in my inbox. And guess what? I opened it straight away.

No subject line. But still a 100% open rate. ;)

Why?

Because I knew who it was from. I was expecting it. And I cared about what was inside.

To get more of your list to open your emails, we don't need to trick our subscribers. Instead:

1. We need to establish trust, to make sure our subscribers are expecting emails from us.
2. Make them remember who we are.
3. Deliver value consistently so they want to read more..

To do these three things is really simple, but perhaps not easy. That's why it's the biggest lever you can pull to get each subscriber to read more of your emails.

For illustration purposes, let's look at #1–making sure people are expecting to hear from us.

That sounds obvious. But think about how you got people on your email list–probably with a lead magnet, by saying 'Would you like this free thing?'

Play this out in your mind - someone sees your lead magnet and it's something they really want. They see they can have it for free if they give you their email address.

So they enter it and hit submit.

They receive the free gift.

And as far as they're concerned, the transaction is complete.

They paid with their email address. That was the currency.

And they *received* it.

Loop complete.

But then they start getting all these emails from you. Emails they weren't expecting.

That's one situation. Of course, everyone is savvy to this kind of thing now so it's more likely that they *are* expecting your emails. And they know that's just a price they pay for getting the free thing.

Instead let's switch this to actually 'sell' the value of your emails themselves so they are expecting them because you said you're going to send them.

You remove the suspicion on that sign up page because you call it out with something like:

Get Our XYZ Thing for Free When You Join Our Email Newsletter Today.

Join 140,000 People who get our daily dose of inspiration about SUBJECT free.
Just enter your name and email:

Not only do your open rates go up, because they have been sold on the benefits and expectation of getting your emails, but your opt-in rate can go up too because you're being honest and removing that suspicion which causes more friction.

Now, let's think about #2–they need to remember *who* you are.

This is arguably much tougher than many of us think at first.

On average, we each receive 121 mails every day from different people. We then see more and more people on social media. Some names we know, some we don't.

That means remembering who you are is really, really hard.

There's a two-part solution to this...

Step One: Email regularly so they don't have time to forget about you.

If someone doesn't hear from you at least every three days, they're absolutely forgetting who you are. You're becoming just another unknown name in their inbox.

Email every three days *minimum*. We email every day. That's not for everyone.

It could be.

It *should* be.

And since subscribers joined your email list to get help solving a problem, your emails will be welcomed into their inbox because you're sharing how you can help them.

It takes less than 20 minutes a day for you to send an email, especially when you plan the hooks and stories first (more on that later), but it's a tough thing to initially commit to. I get that.

My point is, once you have your email frequency set at every 3 days or better, people will remember who you are.

Step Two: Make yourself more identifiable. The first thing people read when an email lands is not the subject line. It's the 'From' name. So, how do you make sure they recognise you? You change the 'From' name in your email system to be your name followed by your brand or what you do.

You want to get the open rate for the reputation YOU have built with your subscribers.

Let's say you have a regular, common name like Jack. (Your last name might be unique but who really remembers last names? Not me. I don't even have one... ;))

You want to make sure that when YOUR emails land in their inbox, they recognise you and don't confuse you with a different 'Jack' whose emails suck, are super-long, have tricky subject lines and are boring. You *need* people to know for sure that it's you and not Boring Jack.

So, you change the 'From' name.

For example, if your name is Carol and you teach flower arranging, your 'From' name might look like this:

>Carol | Flower Arranging School

Even me, with a fairly unique name, when I send our emails out, it comes from:

>Kennedy // Email Marketing Heroes

You can format this however you like best. For some inspiration, here are some other formats that our students use:

>Lillian (A Star Music)
>Jon : Bass Guitar Lessons
>Andy [Junior Martial Arts]
>David ⌐ Youth Offender Bible Studies ⌐
>Karishma @ The Career Coach
>Emma "Marketing Strategist" Louise

Ariel ✏ Nutrition Coaching
Karl // Male Performance
Toni - Dyslexic Readers
Andreas
(Teaches horse-riding so uses an emoji about his niche)
Benita = Build Your Tax Firm
Dan ▶ Sobriety Coach

As you can see, you can get pretty creative to stand out.

Pick one that suits you (and check your email system allows for emojis in the 'From' name if you're going to use one of those).

Well, that was a long chapter. But if I lost you along the way, what you need to take from it is simple: the best way to make sure your subscribers recognise you is by *increasing email frequency* and *making yourself more identifiable*.

ACTIONS:

1. **Tell people they'll join your email newsletter when opting in, so getting your emails is expected, not a surprise.**

2. **Email more often so people remember who you are and form a deeper relationship with you.**

3. **Don't trick people into opening your emails with sneaky subject lines, because that kills long term relationships with your subscribers.**

4. **Use Compound Curiosity for better, original subject lines.**

(Funny bonus idea: write subject lines that when read together in reverse order tell a story so when they are read together in the inbox they say something - I might do that for a laugh some time. You can try it, too, and let me know what you do with it...)

PSYCH STACKED EMAIL MARKETING

Our Top 100 Subject Lines of the Year. Use these as inspiration or just copy them, knowing these subject lines brought in the most clicks and sales.

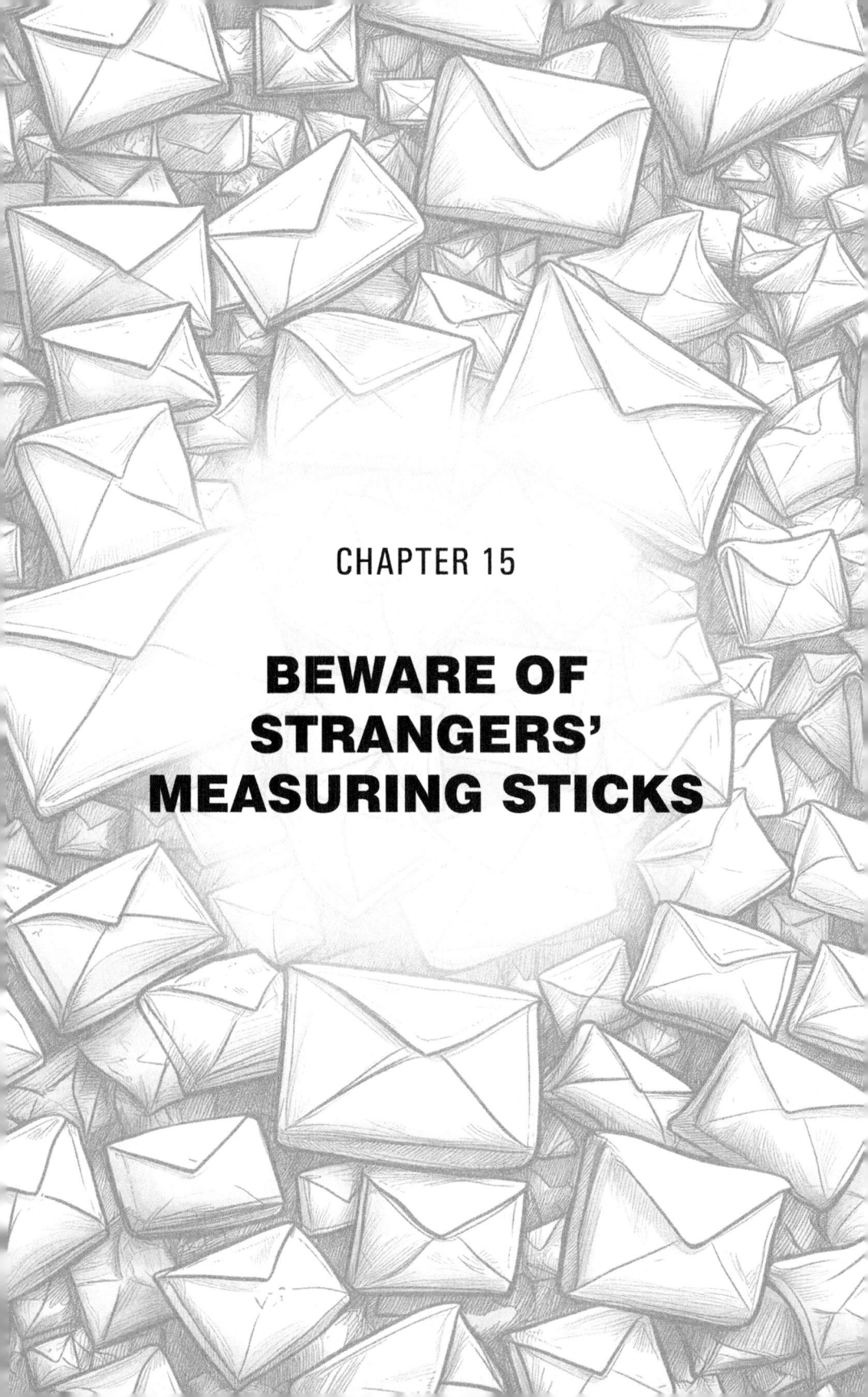

CHAPTER 15

BEWARE OF STRANGERS' MEASURING STICKS

A word of warning: the people who complain that they don't like your emails are not the worst—or the most dangerous.

There is another evil villain we must defeat so you can be the email marketing heroes of your business.

I want to talk to you about responses from your subscribers. As you send emails, some people will reply directly, some will message you privately, and some will even let you know in real life.

The truth is, the strategies you've learned in this book get results. But as you implement them, you might get feedback.

One of our clients, Anne, attended an in-person networking event and someone came up to her and said:

"I don't like your emails. I'm sorry, I don't. I've been reading them and they're too salesy, they're just a bit too direct, they seem unfinished…"

I went on a full-on, impassioned, and very sweary rant about this on one of our member Q&A calls.. This is such a hot topic to me that I went hell-for-leather for over seven solid minutes. Mostly without taking a breath.

(I've grabbed the recording from that session and popped it here if you want to go watch it. At the end of that rant, the whole room applauded, thanked me and said they needed to hear that. It's very motivational but it is pretty sweary, too: EmailMarketingBook.com/feedback)

Here's the thing about feedback like this: It's going to happen.

You're going to hear from people who want to tell you they don't like your emails. But the good news? You'll also hear from people who love your emails.

(We'll get to the most dangerous ones in a moment.)

The Problem With Unsolicited Feedback

When you take a bold approach to something, you're going to evoke emotions. That's the point. Without making people feel something, we can't inspire them into action.

In the world of stand-up comedy and variety performance (where I come from), there's a very big, very important rule about feedback.

Unsolicited feedback is not allowed.

It's forbidden.

And I think that should apply to all of life.

Say you're in a comedy club in New York City. There are four comedians on the bill that night.

The first guy comes off stage and goes back to sit with the other acts.

The other acts do NOT give feedback.

They don't offer words of wisdom, help or give suggestions.

Nothing.

Why?

Because the act didn't ask for it.

IF the guy asks for it, then feedback is welcome. But until then, we don't volunteer feedback.

When someone offers you words of wisdom—you know the sort, offered in a caring, usually condescending-as-fuck tone that's designed to make you feel young and small, so the other person can feel superior, older and smarter—they're not qualified to give you that feedback.

Let me repeat: *They're not qualified.*

They don't know your purpose.

They don't know your strategy.

They don't know your intention.

And they don't know your _**results**_.

You're going to try things from this book and some people won't like them.

But what matters most? That you're not to a subscribers' taste, or the extra sales coming in each day?

Different Measuring Sticks

My mam wouldn't like my emails.

My sister wouldn't like my emails.

My high school English teacher, Miss Hudsun, would _fucking hate_ my emails.

You know who does like them?

- My accountant.
- The tax man.
- Me, when I'm flying business class to Las Vegas to watch shows and staying in 5-star hotels. Me, when I'm bringing on new team members. Me, when I can see all of the amazing people I'm helping.

I like my emails.

Let's look at ome of the feedback you might get, so you're prepared instead of being discouraged.

"Your emails feel unfinished."

What is this person talking about? It turned out that they were referring to the welcome campaign we use called Getting to Know You.

They were referring to the fact the emails end with things like, 'And tomorrow, I'm going to show you....'

They thought the emails were incomplete.

They were correct, but for the wrong reason.

The emails *purposefully* end like that to drive the reader to read the next email. That's the point.

But this person doesn't know that. So she's unqualified to tell me whether my emails are good or not.

They're good according to the measuring stick *I* am using.

She has a different measuring stick.

She's reading the emails from the point of view of a nice piece of learning, a book, or something– I don't know *what*. But my measuring stick is the level of engagement in those emails. And the Getting to Know

You sequence that we use and teach gets an insane level of opens and clicks.

My measuring stick is a happy stick, thank you very much.

And I also start sentences with the word 'and' - like this one. I start bloody paragraphs with 'and' too.

I swear in my emails.

I change tense midway through a sentence or paragraph.

I start thoughts and go off on tangents.

But we're not trying to impress an exam board, our parents, or anyone for that matter.

I'm writing with a purpose. And outsiders don't know what that purpose is or how well it's working for you.

Not so long ago, we got a 1-star review on our podcast, *The Email Marketing Show*. 1 star.

And the person went on to say something about us being too much fun and they wish we'd just get into the content.

I imagine they then promptly melted like a snowflake, dripping onto any of the other boring AF podcasts.

They're right. We spend around six minutes at the start of every episode fannying about, having a laugh and sharing what's going on in our personal lives.

Is that by accident? I mean, you know me pretty well by now, so you know it's not by accident.

The start of the podcast is about rapport, it's about letting all of our listeners in to learn about me personally. You find out my likes, dislikes and weird facts about me.

I had a complaint once that I was 'too much' and I go 'too far'.

That was from a friend.

The first thing that makes me laugh about both of these situations is that these are usually the same people who are advocating for people to show up as their genuine selves and be 'authentic'.

Fuck, just writing the word makes me gag.

The problem with these people, notice it's a problem with them and not me or us or you, is that they want you to be authentic as long as it aligns with *their* beliefs and feelings.

But don't you dare say something that crosses a line or, dare I say, 'triggers' them.

Mate, I get 'triggered' every day. It's part of being a person. It's part of living.

I'll see anything to do with dads and immediately I miss Dad and flash back to sitting next to his hospital bed as he passes away.

Every fucking day.

These flakes are giving lip service to 'being authentic'. Because the truth is, they might not like the real you.

And that's okay.

So what did I say to 'be less fun'?

I was authentic! I said, I'd rather not have a podcast than cut those things out. "There's thousands of boring podcasts, you can go listen to them."

If they don't like your free emails, they can unsubscribe. After all, you're including the link in your emails every time you send one. They may as well make use of it.

When you send an email you're not going round to their house, knocking on their door and eating their biscuits.

They joined YOUR email list.

And just like if they came to yours and said I don't like dogs and cats, and I don't like the colour of the walls -

you'd let them know they can piss off and leave.

They joined *your* email list. They can leave at any point if they don't like it.

But this is of course with the proviso that you are seeing the results you want. And using everything you have now learned from this book you'll be able to do just that.

rant over

The Most Dangerous Feedback

After that tangent…let's go back to the most *dangerous* people.

You see, the people who tell you they don't like your emails are not the ones you have to be careful of, not by a long mile. It's quite easy to say fuck 'em to people who disagree and don't understand. But this next bunch are much easier to fall foul of.

And this one might surprise you…

It's the people who reply to your emails and come up to you to tell you that they love them.

"OMG I love your emails."

"I always read them."

"They're so valuable."

This feedback feels great. It strokes your ego. It convinces you that what you're doing is effective.

But let's go back to our goal with sending these emails.

Just like we're not trying to please our English teachers, we're also not writing novels that are meant to be enjoyed. The sole and only purpose of email marketing is to move people towards a sale.

Someone might have a fantastic weekly newsletter packed with valuable, well-researched articles. But unless your business is the Newsletter Model–where you provide value in the way a newspaper does, and then monetise through advertising and sponsorship deals–that's not the goal.

We're talking about email marketing that makes sales.

Now, I'm not saying you need to get no feedback, and getting positive feedback is a bad thing.

Just like negative feedback, it's just feedback. And it's *still* unsolicited.

We get contacted every day by people saying how much they love our emails. And that is a really lovely thing that we do enjoy. Of course. Who's not enjoying a compliment? We're human and deeply crippled with self doubt.

But if those subscribers aren't clicking and buying, it doesn't matter. Both styles of feedback are separate to the effectiveness of email marketing.

I'm not saying kick these people off your list. After all, if they're opening, clicking and replying to your emails they are really helping with your email deliverability (I'll cover that another time).

But don't be using their opinions to steer what you should and should not be doing. This can be tricky because some of these people tend to have the loudest voices. Remember to do more of what makes people buy.

Our email marketing is extremely effective. Not by the feelings of being liked versus disliked. But by the *results*. By how much we generate from the email list.

That is the only thing that matters.

ACTION:
Decide, early on, the results you want from your campaigns. Then measure the success of any marketing activity on the metrics that matter, not on opinions of other people - good or bad. Only on the results *you* want.

Entrepreneur's Flight Deck is my personal dashboard of numbers that every business should be tracking so you can measure your growth and be sure you have clear eyes on the numbers that tell you whether you're on track to reach your goals, what is failing, what needs attention, what is working so you can do more of it. Get my whole flight deck to manage your journey using this QR code:

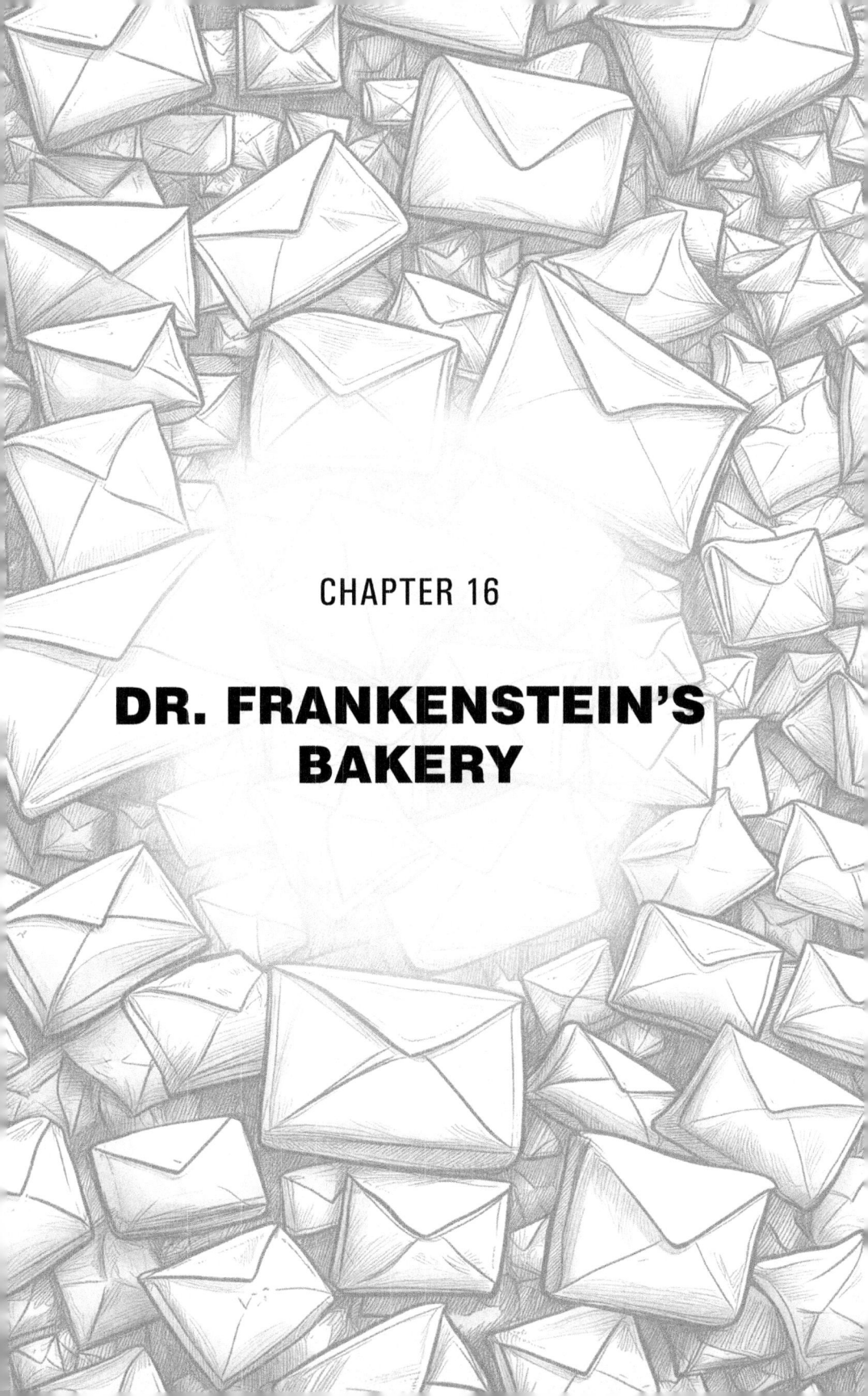

CHAPTER 16

DR. FRANKENSTEIN'S BAKERY

What you've got now is a practical method to significantly increase sales from both your current and future email subscribers.

You now understand that:

- **All roads lead to Rome.** This creates a compounding effect on sales across your whole business.

- **Help people buy, don't nurture them to death.** Your goal is to guide them to the best solution to their problem, not overwhelm them with endless 'nurturing' emails.

- **Having a sales sequence early on legitimises future offers.** Introducing your product upfront in a subscribers' journey makes later discounts and bonuses feel natural, not desperate.

- **Copywriting isn't the game-changer.** If we want to create significant sales from our email lists, we need to start pulling on big levers like context, hooks, emphases, structure, and strategy.

- **Consistency builds momentum when it comes to offers.** To maximise sales, we need to stick with an offer for longer instead of moving onto the next offer and the next one.

- **Shorter emails with a single focus connect better.** Readers engage more when each email delivers a clear point.

- **Design campaigns first, then fit the tech to them.** Never let software dictate your marketing strategy.

- **People buy for different reasons.** Your campaigns should appeal to various buying motivations, not just one.

- **Recognition and reputation trump subject lines.** People open emails from senders they trust, not just because of catchy (or misleading) subject lines.

- **Unsolicited feedback is unacceptable.** Enough said.

- **I hate Where's-Wally/Waldo.** Also, enough said.

A lot of what we've shared with you here is a totally different way to think about your email marketing. This is only for the brave people who are willing to try going against what all those generic email marketing lessons have taught them.

Some of this is uncomfortable. We get it. We hear about it every day from our students. But it's in stretching yourself and pushing yourself to do new things that you're about to achieve new things and climb new summits.

The Danger of 'Frankenstein-ing' Your Strategy

At this point, many people will be tempted to do what we call 'Frankenstein-ing'.

Take Lucas, for example. He came to one of our coaching sessions for some personalized input on his webinar strategy.

He went on to tell us that he was using Russell Brunson's this, and Frank Kern's that, Amy Porterfield's other thing, and something else he saw my friend Natalie Ellis at Boss Babe doing.

Woah. Woah-woah.

Pause.

Stop.

Step away from the keyboard.

I hear this a lot. Most of us do this, don't we? We take bits of what we're learning from people and assemble them into something that *feels* right. That's Frankenstein-ing.

The problem? If you take *pieces* of other people's proven strategies you end up with NO PROVEN STRATEGY.

What if all the bits you choose are the bits that don't matter?

The whole point of a strategy is that it's more than the sum of its parts. Each part of a five-part strategy might contribute 10% toward the success of it. But it's the compounding nature of those pieces–in *that* order, done in *that* way–that takes it from 50% to 100%.

Follow, Then Innovate

So how *do* you implement things?

1. **Start with emulation.** Follow a strategy exactly as intended. No changes, no tweaks

2. **Get results first.** Once you see some successes, , you can start tweaking things to see if you can move the needle to make it better.

3. **Optimize for your business.** Beyond conversions, focus on how it suits you, feels to you, fits with how and what you want to do.

Let's go back to the webinar example. You might start off following Person X's live webinar strategy, but your ultimate goal is to make it automated. So, you:

- Run the live webinar exactly as Person X teaches.
- Do it five or six times before you dial it in.
- Only then do you start applying things to make it evergreen.

It's like baking a cake. If you skip the eggs, you can't be totally surprised when the cake is a flop.

Same applies for your email marketing strategy.

The impact and results are far greater than the sum of the ingredients.

Stick with the strategy.

Why My Approach Works

What makes my email marketing methods different from the rest?

Simple: I obsess over email marketing and nothing else.

When something works, we double down on it. The more we refine it, the deeper our expertise gets.

We're up to our eyes in email marketing. We constantly test, analyse, and optimise based on real-world results.

By questioning everything, we've made email marketing work on a whole new level that gets results at this whole new level. Which is what is needed.

It's our mission to totally overhaul email marketing so that we all—as subscribers—receive better emails and actually enjoy the emails we get. And that, as businesses, we get to send emails we like.

It's the type of email marketing that doesn't make you want to be sick in your own mouth.

The old techniques of banging people over the head with sales messages until they "buy die or unsubscribe" can't get us there. Sending 'value' that adds to our overwhelm and takes a load of time to produce, *won't get us there.*

A radically different approach is needed.

An approach that doesn't just duct tape tricks and tactics together, but instead a singular strategic approach where every single element is meticulously designed to fit together like pieces of a jigsaw puzzle to create a whole picture that is greater than the sum of its parts.

ACTION:

Don't pick and choose parts of different strategies. Stick to one strategy and make it work, before making 'improvements'.

RESOURCES AND MORE

So, if you want to learn more about our training, get our actual email campaigns (there's more than 45 different ones for everything you could want to do, and a lot of inspiration for things that you could do) you can try some of these routes, we'd love to stay in touch and we'd love to help you do this faster and better with our shortcuts and guidance:

1. Our flagship "Rome" product is our Automated Email Engine. This is the whole thing on Email Marketing. That's at EmailMarketingHeroes.com/engine

2. Our free podcast and YouTube show is called *The Email Marketing Show*. Go to YouTube, Apple Podcasts, Spotify, and wherever you get podcasts from and search for it by name. Each week, we have a new episode for you where we talk about what's working right now in email marketing, give you ideas and techniques and of course have a good laugh while doing it. Come listen in.

3. Get all the tools and templates mentioned in this book using the QR code at the end of this chapter.

Finally, can I just say a resounding 'fuck yes!' to the fact you made it to the last page of this book. Not only do most people not see results in most things they try or try things they read, but almost no one even reads the whole book.

What we've shared here is obviously not a guarantee of untold riches or, frankly, any results at all. This is a detailed account of some major principles which we have personally used and that many of our most successful students have used in our businesses with our experience and expertise.

Entrepreneurship is a tough game, and the odds of most people giving up before finding what works for them are high. So, hats off to you for being here.

Now go do some stuff!

KAPOW!!

- Kennedy
EmailMarketingHeroes.com

LOOK WHO'S TALKING - ABOUT THE AUTHOR

Widely recognised as the world's foremost authority on psychology-based email marketing, Kennedy is the creative force behind Email Marketing Heroes, helping digital product creators sell more through their email lists without resorting to gimmicks, hype, or shady tactics.

With over 20 years of experience as a psychological mind reader, performing on stages at high-profile conferences and luxury cruise ships across the globe, Kennedy captivates audiences with his blend of entertainment and expertise. His keynote sessions are the most talked about at conferences, delivering insights that transform how businesses approach email marketing.

Through Email Marketing Heroes, Kennedy has helped more than 8,000 entrepreneurs, giving them the tools and confidence to turn even the tiniest email lists into consistent revenue streams. Known for his no-nonsense, psychology-over-technology approach, he's built a 7-figure-a-year online business with fewer than 5,000 active subscribers. His mission? To help experts make more sales of their courses, memberships, and coaching programs—all while staying true to their voice and values.

Kennedy's ideas and strategies have been praised by industry leaders and have earned him a reputation for being refreshingly practical and hilariously relatable. Kennedy is pawrent to two Bengal cats—Nova and Ivy—and feels awkward AF about writing this in the third person.

ACKNOWLEDGEMENTS AND THANKS

Writing this book started off as a thing I did alone, lying down on my sofa with vertigo. But to take it from ramblings and turn it into something that anyone would want to read, not to mention get value from, it has taken a village of people.

I've been dreading this part because now I have to try and list them without missing anyone out. Thanks to:

Alexa Padou my Editor (thanks for not just ripping this apart but for also laughing at my fucked up sense of humour and writing 'so true' in the margins a lot)

Emma Louise

Aidan O'Sullivan

Issy Howell

Todd Brown

Fifi Mason

Shaun Mitchell

IMPLEMENT THESE LESSONS, FAST!

I want you to have everything you need to implement what I've shared in this book. Point your phone camera at the QR code below and get additional materials, SOPs, detailed training that's more actionable stuff than in most $1,997 gugu courses:

Printed in Dunstable, United Kingdom

68243197R00100